SEMIOTEXT(E) INTERVENTION SERIES

© Sergio González Rodríguez, 2014. Originally published in
Spanish by Editorial Anagrama S.A.

Published by Semiotext(e)
PO BOX 629, South Pasadena, CA 91031
www.semiotexte.com

Thanks to John Ebert

Design: Hedi El Kholti

ISBN: 978-1-63590-088-0
Distributed by the MIT Press, Cambridge, Mass.,
and London, England
Printed in the United States of America

Sergio González Rodríguez

Field of Battle

Introduction by David Lida

Translated by Joshua Neuhouser

semiotext(e)
intervention
series □ 27

Contents

Introduction by David Lida

BEYOND COPS AND ROBBERS

Sergio González Rodríguez was a restless drinker.

I remember a typical Friday afternoon we spent together with a couple of friends, not long after we met in the early 2000s. We started with an *aperitivo* in a cantina in the old center of town at about one in the afternoon, an hour or so before anyone in Mexico City thinks about lunch. No sooner had the waiter brought the drinks than Sergio began to think aloud about another cantina a few blocks away, and how much more amusing a place it was than where we were. By the time we arrived to the next cantina, Sergio had already thought of a third place where we needed to have a drink, as soon as we finished the ones that we hadn't even yet ordered in the second. And so it went, through the afternoon and into the evening, when we were bleary-eyed and befuddled, only spasmodically detailing the places we'd been.

All of us except for Sergio. At the time, he wrote a column that appeared every Friday in the newspaper

Reforma, called *Los bajos fondos* (The Lower Depths). In an ironic tone, he reviewed bars, cantinas, discotheques, and virtually any place where you could find a drink in Mexico City. (*Los bajos fondos* was also the title of his first book, published in 1988, an essay about the bohemian underworld of Mexico City in the late 19th and the first half of 20th century.)

Because his knowledge of watering holes in the city was so close to encyclopedic, I always felt a sense of invincibility whenever I took him somewhere he'd never been before. We probably went to eight or ten bars on that Friday excursion. The last stop, at my suggestion, was called Bar Oxford, on the ground floor of the Hotel Oxford, in a tenebrous neighborhood called La Tabacalera (which means cigarette factory—it was the first base of smoking manufacture in Mexico City). The Bar Oxford has changed in the last few years, but back then, most of the customers were traveling salesmen and the odd European backpacker, attracted by the central location and the hotel's inexpensive if rudimentary lodgings. Filling out the cast of characters were itinerant musicians who earned drinks and spare change by wandering from bar to bar and serenading the customers, and corpulent, middle-aged prostitutes, who were given to spreading their arms across the tables and laying their heads atop them on slow evenings.

But this was Friday, the busiest night of the week. Sergio had never been to the Oxford before. We had been drinking for nine hours or so, and as such neither of us was particularly coherent. After one more drink, he disappeared. This was Sergio's modus operandi—he seldom said goodnight, preferring a method known in Mexico City as "the French goodbye." You'd be talking to him one moment, avert your gaze to blow your nose or find something in your pocket, and by the time you turned back to him, he would be gone.

A week later, Sergio's report about the Oxford appeared in *Los bajos fondos*. Despite all the hours we'd spent drinking, the spindly legs on which he stood at the end of the night, and the disjointedness of our conversation by that hour, his description of the place was elegant, nuanced and an absolute bull's eye in its characterization. There were details of the place which he noticed that I, a fairly frequent customer, had never seen.

For a writer known for a proclivity for drink, Sergio was extraordinarily productive. In addition to *Los bajos fondos*, he wrote two articles a week for the arts section at *Reforma*, and was an editorial consultant for the paper's weekly cultural supplement. Before he died at the age of 67 on April 3, 2017, he had written more than 20 books, establishing himself as one of the most important Mexican writers of his generation. He wrote novels, essays and what in Mexico are called *crónicas*, many of which were works of literary journalism that defy characterization and category. The piece of work that made his reputation was *Huesos en el desierto* (Bones in the Desert), published in 2002. Meticulously researched and reported, it was the first book about the serial killings of dozens of women in Ciudad Juárez, Chihuahua, on the Mexican border across the bridge from El Paso, Texas, that began in the mid 1990s. The victims included children and the elderly, although most were in their late teens and early twenties. They'd come to Juárez from all over the Mexican provinces to find work in the piecework factories established there after the North American Free Trade Agreement took effect. They worked twelve-hour shifts on assembly lines making coffee pots, toaster ovens, baby clothes, ironing boards, hospital scrubs and any number of other products that would ultimately be sold in the U.S.

Huesos en el desierto looks at the phenomenon of the murders from distinct angles—the stories of the victims and their families; a hapless immigrant from the Middle East scapegoated for the crimes; members of the police, the armed forces, and representatives of local, state and federal governments, who not only turned a blind eye to whether justice was served but some of whom, according to Sergio's research, may have been actively involved.

The book is typical of his nonfiction in that he is unafraid to point figures at and name the names of the people involved, no matter how powerful.

At the time the book came out, the most popular morning news show on TV was hosted by a comedian named Victor Trujillo who, dressed as a clown called Brozo, conducted fairly hard-hitting discussions of recent events. When Sergio appeared on the show, the host, referring to Sergio's fearlessness at making accusations against such high-level figures, asked him, "*Los tienes bien grandes, ¿verdad?*" (You've got real big ones, right?) Aside from reflecting the Mexican macho's predisposition for valuing his genitals above any other organ, the question posed the real possibility that Sergio could have been killed for writing *Huesos*. Indeed, a couple of years earlier, he paid a heavy price when some fragments of the book were published in *Reforma*. After one piece came out, Sergio was kidnapped by thugs who commandeered a taxi he was riding. They beat him mercilessly, warning that his work was being closely monitored. Despite the cerebral hemorrhage he suffered from the blows to his head, he didn't heed their threats.

In addition to his bravery, Sergio's work was notable for its scope and acuity. I remember a conversation he and I had about a U.S. journalist who published some books about crime and lawlessness in Juárez. Sergio considered him to be an affable and well-intentioned fool: "He still thinks Juárez is a cops-and-robbers story," he said. On the contrary, Sergio's work about Juárez, and all of Mexico in recent years, is much more sophisticated. Through fastidiously sourced analysis, he paints a portrait of Mexico on a geopolitical level, pointing to the links between the failure of the country's leaders to effectively police and adjudicate its criminals, to the government and the armed forces' collusion with those criminals, as well as with the United States government (including the CIA's efforts to destabilize Mexico).

Field of Battle is Sergio's most powerful work about the unholy alliance between Mexico and the U.S., and how the former renders itself utterly to the global political strategies of the latter. It describes the militarization of Mexico's police force, the CIA's involvement with the paramilitary groups that patrol much of Mexico's countryside, and the DEA's designation of Mexican drug traffickers as "Transnational Criminal Organizations" in order to taint them as terrorists rather than drug dealers. He writes that "the suspicion of terrorism radicalizes and loosens the construction of the image of the enemy," allowing for "the indiscriminate use of armed violence in the name of internal security, as well as the unprovoked declaration of war against foreign states, the normalization and institutionalization of states of exception and, lastly, the use of extralegal measures not just in international relations against enemy terrorists, but also within the state itself, as well as in its relations with foreign democracies."

Whenever some issue of Mexican politics mystified me, I'd call Sergio. No matter how complicated the situation, he was capable of breaking it down concisely and quickly. While *Field of Battle* is an indictment of the administration of Enrique Peña Nieto, president of Mexico from 2012 to 2018, it's also quickly proving to foreshadow what's to come. I write this prologue three weeks after Andrés Manuel López Obrador has assumed the presidency. In direct contradiction to his campaign promises, he has already announced the creation of a fifty-thousand-member militia to be known as the National Guard, to be trained by the Army, increasing the militarization of Mexico. With a caravan of thousands of immigrants from Central America at the Tijuana border trying to cross into the U.S., López Obrador's administration hasn't said a word against its northern neighbor, even after it threw canisters of tear gas at the immigrants trying to make it to the other side of the San Ysidro crossing. Defying its own Immigration and Nationality Act, the U.S. is denying entry to asylum seekers, even those who can demonstrate a credible fear of returning to their countries, obliging them to remain in Mexico. How I wish I could ask

Sergio over drinks in a cantina what he makes of all this.

* * *

He was born in Mexico City in 1950. Sergio's mother died when he was in the third grade, and, as he wrote in his posthumously published book *Teoría novelada de mí mismo* (Novelized Theory of Myself), not long after her death, his father formed another family, effectively leaving Sergio and his siblings to fend for themselves. (Sergio would remain devoted to his brothers and sisters, as well as his nieces and nephews, until his death.) He studied English literature at the country's most important school, the National Autonomous University of Mexico, and in his youth played electric bass in a beloved hard rock band called Enigma, alongside some of his brothers. As long as I knew him, he wore a hearing aid, and claimed that he became a journalist after too much abuse to his eardrums in his musical years.

He could speak and write with authority about writers as diverse as Marcel Proust and Henry James, Juan Rulfo and Adolfo Bioy Casares, Georges Bataille and Gilles Deleuze, E. M. Cioran and Walter Benjamin, J. G. Ballard and Philip K. Dick. He also had an exhaustive knowledge of film (he loved the guilty pleasure of escaping to the movies by himself in the middle of an afternoon), and had formidable knowledge about art, design and architecture. Late in life he obtained a law degree from a university in Spain, and was invited to lecture about Mexico all over Europe.

As a sort of counterpoint to his intellect, Sergio was strongly sentimental. I never saw him happier than when perusing the offerings of a juke box. I remember tears coming to his eyes one night when I played CDs of my favorite Dinah Washington songs for him at my apartment.

In the late 1990s, he befriended the Chilean novelist Roberto Bolaño, who had lived in Mexico City during his adolescence in the 1970s, but never again returned. Much of Bolaño's work is set in Mexico, and the Chilean had frequent conversations with Sergio, who filled in the half-remembered details of so many years before. In his novel *2666*, Bolaño invented the character of a journalist named Sergio González Rodríguez, who operates from a northern Mexican city, investigating the murders of innocent women. Despite the name and premise, the character bears little resemblance to Sergio. I frequently joked with him that I preferred Bolaño's version to the real thing, although in truth Sergio was much more complex than Bolaño's creation. He also appears as a character in the Spanish writer Javier Marías's "false novel" *Negra espalda del tiempo*.

During the last few years of his life, I saw Sergio less frequently than I had in the previous decade or so. He'd been in an accident while riding his bicycle, and had other health problems, including a form of bone disease, about which he was vague, claiming it was neither osteoporosis or osteopenia. We exchanged frequent emails and text messages. Once in a while he would call out of the blue, usually in the late afternoon or early evening, and curtly ask, "What are you doing?"

"Working," I'd say, or "Having coffee with a friend," or whatever activity I was engaged in at the moment.

"Come over here," he'd say, without bothering to mention where he was. "All I'm asking for is a half hour of your time."

I was seldom able to take the bait when he wanted me to drop everything and come to see him. Sometimes we'd make a formal plan to get together, and he'd always propose that we meet for *algo leve*—something mild. We'd connect for lunch in a restaurant, usually in the neighborhood where I lived. He'd order a tequila as an *aperitivo* before eating. We'd share a bottle of wine during the meal, and afterwards he'd have a "43," a Spanish liqueur, as a *digestivo*. Once he'd had enough of that treacle, he'd suggest we repair to my place, where he knew I always had a bottle of bourbon stashed. Sometimes he'd produce some other narcotic to accompany the whiskey.

Sergio was one of the most generous people I have ever met, with his time, his money, his contacts and resources. In the world of Mexico City journalism, he opened doors for many reporters who came from other parts of the country, or, like me, from even further afield. I remember his extreme indignation about one of these people, which he expressed one night in a cantina. He'd assigned to this writer an article for *Reforma*, and the guy—to whom Sergio had virtually handed the journalistic keys to the city—told Sergio that he couldn't write it. He was now beholden to another editor, a man notoriously jealous of Sergio's success, and this editor forbade him to contribute to any media with which Sergio was involved.

Sergio thought it was the height of ingratitude. Again, tears came to his eyes when he told the story. After he calmed down, he said, "Don't worry. The good guys will win." At first I was astounded by the remark: Was Sergio, so worldly, well-read and sophisticated, breaking us all down to good guys and bad guys, seeing the world as reductively as the U.S. journalist who painted Juárez as a cops-and-robbers story? On reflection, I realized he wasn't. Sergio may have been brilliant, he may have been courageous, he may have been a great writer, and he was certainly the best drinking companion in Mexico City. But he was above all a decent human being, and his lament was that this quality was in short supply among our colleagues and contemporaries. I had one brother, who died of AIDS in 1992. When Sergio died last year, I felt as if I had lost another.

THE NOTION OF A FIELD

A sizable parcel in a rural area, an undeveloped lot in an urban environment, a plot of arable land, a plain as opposed to a hill or mountain, a place for games and recreational activities, a site for duels, an area of academic study: these are some of the accepted meanings of the word *field*. And there are also electric fields, magnetic fields, fields of vision, fields in space, fields where research is conducted, fields occupied by an army during wartime.

In many parts of the world, this last meaning—the theater of war—represents the concept and reality of the field as it intersects with the lives of individuals, geopolitics, military strategy, the artistic and cultural spheres and the control and surveillance of collectives. Here we must talk of the strategic plan for the militarization of the world, the global model of control and surveillance and the field of battle in Mexico at the beginning of the 21st century, a case in which we can see a variety of factors, agents, circumstances, processes and trends that are far from being unique in the world.

On the contrary, these factors express the forms through which the concepts and procedures employed by nation-states under the existing global-local order emerge and consolidate themselves in every corner of the world: ultracontemporariness, which refers to the space/time of globalization (simultaneous, ubiquitous, systemic and productive) and includes historical-local time and the notion of "real time," which has been borrowed from the world of information and communications technology (the Internet, in particular), as well as the trend towards the use of English as the lingua franca of the entire world. A comprehensive flattening of the civilian and military spheres, respecting neither borders nor any other limitations.[1]

The subject under examination here is something latent, gestating or explicitly present in many societies, as they share the same economic base and the same sociopolitical system: formal democracy of the ultraliberal type within the framework of a globalized economy and a militaristic/technocratic security model, as was established during the last two decades of the 20th century. This model includes drug trafficking as a military target, comparable to terrorism or insurgency.[2]

In their limitations in terms of justice, equality and the distribution of wealth, quality of life and future opportunities for the majority of the population, states and countries on every continent show warning signs for large-scale conflicts and continuous social crises that transcend the scope of political science, criminology and the diplomatic bureaucracy. It is urgent that we understand the comprehensive transformation of our civilization that this implies: the era of a technological-military transhumanism on a planetary scale. The surveillance and control of future societies.

In any general field of studies, there are social contradictions, symbolic structures, rules of domination and mutual influences among participants and institutions, as well as the respective degrees of autonomy between them.[3] In examining the state of emergency at hand, we must include all of these factors and, more decisively, scrutinize the interaction of the energies, forces, pressures and tensions that run through them, reconfiguring them into a reflection of themselves.

A field of battle, in particular, expresses the transition from international conflict to the internalization of conflict within a country's borders. And it reflects a rejection of norms and the institutions that uphold them. An ultracontemporary field of battle is continuous, flat, ubiquitous, systemic and productive, with operations at sea, in the air, on land, in outer space and cyberspace.

The field of battle examined herein transcends Mexican territory, extending across its northern and southern borders, as North America extends itself towards Central America and the Caribbean: the U.S. Northern Command (NORTHCOM) expands outwards in a continuous field of military operations that encompasses the rest of the world. This process of militarization goes back to the last decade of the 20th century and, by 2014, includes *focos* of risk in North Korea, Syria, Ukraine and Venezuela, to name just a few.[4]

This book is a report on the genesis and evolution of the field of battle in the case of Mexico, offering a warning for other countries and continents subject to the inertia of geopolitics and the great transformations at the planetary level. The direct purpose of this report is to provide information through a text that describes, analyzes and illustrates all characteristics and circumstances of an event or issue. And it aspires to clarity and exactness.[5]

A report is something more than a mere narrative or chronicle (chronological history): it inspects and analyzes all aspects of a reality in terms of the bodies (persons), spaces, forms, cartographies and relationships that make up a society in crisis, a war or a state of emergency. And it is committed to acting as a truthful connection between what is registered and studied and what has occurred, daring to offer this connection to other observers or readers. Field, field of exception, field of battle, a report on a field of battle under the current global order.

1

POSTNATIONAL MAP

The shadow of instability that fell over Mexico between 1994 and the dawn of the 21st century needs to be rethought.[1] The map that we have been taught of the Mexican Republic has been transformed into something else entirely: the country in the form of a horn of plenty overflowing with natural resources, a common patriotic symbol in Latin America, belongs to the past.[2] The postnational state that has arisen in its place has imposed a new order. The Pacific and Atlantic coasts and the northern and southern borders have become porous and translinear, opening, closing and readjusting themselves to accommodate the intrusions of the terrestrial and aerial surveillance of the U.S. Army or the convergent activities of organized crime. The U.S., in turn, imposes its hegemony in the arms market.[3]

When power becomes space, it organizes a territory in the form of a map. To have a map is to understand spatial organization: a map provides a

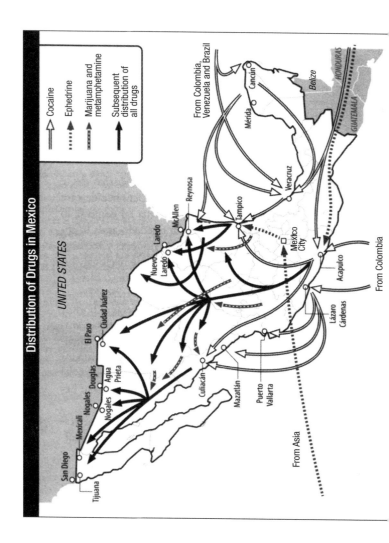

Distribution of Drugs in Mexico

focus for the conjuncture of realities and possibilities for domination. Strategic thinking involves observing things from above and within, seeing through them and beyond them.[4]

The country's regions have been modified by the domination of criminal groups whose drug trafficking activities have reconfigured the map of the country's interior with their transportation routes, temporary conquests and struggles against their competitors, and even in their control and management of common crime and other illegal industries: kidnapping, extortion, theft, human trafficking, child pornography, prostitution, gun running, protection rackets, etc. This territorial dislocation has given rise to a new, constantly shifting cartography that has little to do with traditional maps.[5]

The greatest internal and external transformations have been seen on the Gulf Coast, which links Mexico to Central America through a corridor whose territory and population have been ravaged by crimes against the objectives of human development, sustainability, natural disaster prevention, tourism, the formal economy, trade and the development of energy, transportation and communication infrastructure. The informal, underground economy tends to impose itself in this new, asymmetric configuration: the tunnel.[6]

A territory of human exploitation: those who are expelled from their communities by poverty and criminality and those exiles traveling through Mexico to find work in the United States are abused, killed, raped and extorted at the hands of criminal organizations, suffering from the absence of the rule of law and a lack of respect for human dignity. A vast area that has become a prison, a field that concentrates all the depravation of perverse powers.

This process of dissolution began decades ago in the country's northern border cities and then spread to the rest of the country, whose central, western, northern Pacific and southern regions have witnessed permanent crises and tensions between legality and illegality, creating alegal conditions: even the institutions act outside the law and violate the law.

Every city in these regions has strayed from its old political-administrative statutes based around the rule of law, reformulating themselves under the influence of organized crime and its arrangements with federal, state and local governments. The damage done to the residents of these cities is twofold: expulsion or exile in search of refuge and better living conditions[7] or submission and coercion under the new criminal-institutional order. The rise of the penitentiary model of urban government, in which the strongest and the most corrupt—criminals colluding with government officials—are the ones who exercise political power in society.

The traditional spheres of the public and the private have been subverted: the population, deprived of its rights, lives under a reign of daily terror in which one's private life can become public at any moment through an act of illegal aggression. And prospects for survival have become dire: work, family, belief and community lose their continuity. It is increasingly difficult to reassemble this fragmentation and construct a viable future apart from that ruled by crime and the fight against it.

Mexico has become a field of battle under the new world order and the geopolitical strategy of the United States, the world's greatest superpower. A field subject to the sharpest contradictions.

Nearly all crimes go unpunished in Mexico; its territory, borders and coasts are besieged by criminal groups that challenge the state's monopoly of violence. Extortion and kidnapping have become widespread as Mexico fails to fully implement the Palermo Convention against Transnational Organized Crime. This speaks to the absence of the rule of law.[8]

The assassinations of dozens of journalists in recent years underscores Mexico's pervasive impunity.[9] It's useless to take comfort in statistical relativism, arguing that a difference of 80%, 93% or 99% impunity, versus 100%, indicates that the rule of law exists in Mexico, backed up as it is by an institutional (dis)order that implies the *de facto* rule of drug cartels over large swathes of territory. Or worse still, to point out that other parts of the world also have high rates of impunity: such arguments express the unreason of inept comparativism.

In Mexico, as elsewhere, there is a formalist understanding of the institutions, whose dysfunctionality reveals the dissimulation that rules our public life, a dissimulation in which the entire state takes part, from political parties to the Supreme Court, from governors to senators to deputies, from stockbrokers to media monopolies, from security forces to the criminal justice system, from the electoral cycle to the intellectuals and propagandists that lend their legitimacy to this dissimulation. At the center of all this, society is increasingly vulnerable in the face of the complicity—whether by commission or by omission—of the political and economic powers with organized crime.

The rule of law is an essential and indicative concept for measuring the divide between legality and illegality. Its reference point is centered less on a metalegal principle of abstract law than in the concrete performance of government institutions.

The preponderance of legality indicates the legitimacy of a state, just as the influence of illegality puts into question legality as such as well as a state's alleged legitimacy. From this point of equilibrium, a partial loss of legality in a state's territory formally

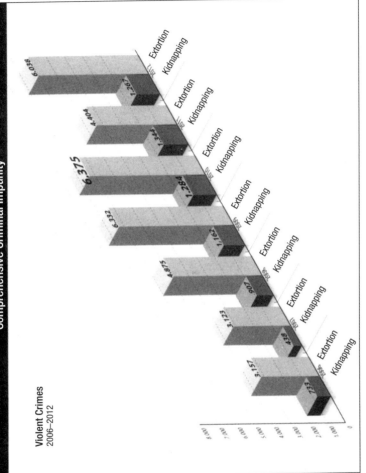

Violent Crimes
2006–2012

and concretely implies a collapse of the rule of law. We use euphemisms when speaking of states in crisis, uselessly trying to alleviate the situation by relativizing it: "fragile state," "weak state," "failed state," "collapsed state," etc.

Under the rule of law, the constitution guarantees the rigidity of legal principles and the "established constitutional rights that specifically limit the powers of the state."[10] The constitution would thus be located at the apex of the legal structure, in a superordinate and normative position with respect to the rest of the legal system.

A constitutional state with the rule of law would be a rights-based state, which means "a model of law, not just of criminal law, but of law in general, oriented towards guaranteeing subjective rights."[11] This means the universality of basic rights. A state that fails to follow its constitutional precepts, therefore, is a lawless state, even if its executive, legislative and judicial branches adhere to a legal formalism. To argue otherwise is to live in a fantasy world. This is the case in Mexico, where the authorities ignore and threaten constitutional principles even in their proposed legal reforms, which are imposed with the complicity of the legislative branch. It is not a coincidence that, in these terms, the constitutional rule of law is associated with democracy, which would be its ideal consequence.[12]

To understand the dysfunctionality of the alleged constitutional state and the absence of the rule of law in Mexico, we need to examine the rupture between formal structures and material reality.

The World Justice Project's International Rule of Law Index[13] indicates that Mexico's profile is heterogeneous and destructive: while the country has a long tradition of constitutional rule (including protections for the freedom of expression and the freedom of religion) and enjoys judicial independence and a liberal regulatory environment, there is a high level of corruption at all levels of government and in the country's security forces; according to this index, the criminal justice system is "deficient" (coming in 63rd place among the 66 countries evaluated), criminal investigations are weak and there is widespread discrimination against marginalized groups, corruption of judges and police officers, and violations of the rights of the accused (here Mexico comes in 64th place). Furthermore, there has been a failure to imprison corrupt police officers and government functionaries (59th place). In general, 91% of common crimes are not reported because of the ineptness and inefficiency of the authorities.[14]

Theory of the a-state: in Mexico, due to the absence of the constitutional rule of law, the state's autocorrective ability is increasingly nonexistent, and

The A-State and Its Behavior

THE MEXICAN STATE

Illegal

Legal

In the a-state, legality and illegality coexist, and this dysfunctionality is supported by the de facto powers that simulate legality and legitimacy

this anomaly has become productive: a *de facto* framework has arisen in which legality and illegality come together under the shadow of a normative state. This situation can be conceptualized as a state that simulates legality and legitimacy while constituting an a-state (from the prefix *a/an*, derived from the Greek ἀ): the absence and negation of itself.

The dysfunctionality of the Mexican a-state feeds off of larger dysfunctionalities, above all the compulsion to pass more and more laws and harsher and harsher punishments instead of focusing on the implementation of existing laws, regulations and constitutional principles. In Mexico, as in many other nations, there is a culture of alegality.

The violence committed in recent years against Mexico's institutions has a common source: the superinstitutional pact that arose from the criminal ties between drug traffickers and the political and economic powers. In Mexico, the concept of the pact goes back thirty years, when pacts or alliances became widespread within the country's oligarchy as a means of reaffirming its strength in the face of the modernization process, above all in the economic sphere.

In the imaginary of its participants, the pact became the ideal mechanism for founding a new order that, in the end, created more problems than it solved. In particular, the arrangements made with criminal organizations under the rule of the Institutional Revolutionary Party (PRI) instituted a division of the country's territory that would last until the early years of the 21st century.[15]

In public life, the concept of the pact has been discredited by its disastrous history for at least two reasons: a) it leads to situations that favor special interests to the detriment of the civilian majority, and b) it covers up illicit or irregular conduct in such a way that the distinction between legality and illegality has been erased.

The gray area in which Mexico's institutional degradation occurred was an imitation of the U.S. government's own ambivalent interactions with organized crime. On the one hand, the United States has punished criminal activities under a framework of due formalism; on the other, certain government agencies have engaged in illegal operations, kept secret from their peers, that violate the country's own laws and, of course, those of others, all in the name of "national security."

In 2012, a 2007 Drug Enforcement Agency (DEA) operation was uncovered in which cocaine was trafficked to Europe from Mexican territory and millions of dollars of illicit origin were transported around the world and laundered in U.S. and Chinese banks. That same year, it was also learned that the Central Intelligence Agency (CIA) was trafficking Bolivian cocaine in Chile, the profits of which were used to destabilize the government of Ecuador. On the pretext of infiltrating criminal organizations, illegality has been legitimized by cross-border activities that undermine the supremacy of the law.[16]

To date, the CIA maintains ties to criminal organizations, destabilizing Mexico under a paramilitary logic.[17] This geopolitical factor falls under the purview of the Mérida Initiative, a product of the Security and Prosperity Partnership of North America (SPP): "A series of policies, regulatory realignments and standards designed to meet security goals both within and outside the region," which tend to impose themselves above the highest law of the land: constitutional principles.[18] The SPP was relabeled the North American Leaders' Summit in 2006 for diplomatic reasons[19] and its policies, which obey NORTHCOM directives, are: 1) to strengthen the Mexican state as a guarantee of the national security of the United States against the threats of organized crime and terrorism from Central America and the Caribbean, and 2) to strengthen and professionalize Mexico's armed forces so they can be used for U.S. national security programs and plans in the future.

In military terms, these directives form part of the great transformation from the industrial era to the era of military intelligence, which the U.S. government began to implement at the end of the 20th century. This is a process that involves reconfiguring military competition and cooperation through new combinations of concepts, capabilities, personnel and organizations that exploit the advantages of the United States in order to protect the country from asymmetrical threats—or unconventional threats, such as terrorism, sabotage and attacks on civilian targets—and maintain a strategic position in the name of world peace and global stability.[20]

To the extent that the U.S. Army has undergone this transformation, it has developed a particular interest in making arrangements for international military cooperation to ensure that changes in its capabilities can be effectively applied in coordination with allied and coalition capabilities: "U.S. transformation objectives should thus be used to shape and complement foreign military developments and priorities of likely partners, both in bilateral and multilateral contexts."[21] Under this military logic, conflicting practices and procedures should be eliminated.

To achieve these objectives, the U.S. government, through the CIA, has carried out "activities" (covert operations) that stimulate *focos* of institutional destabilization in Mexican territory through actions involving organized crime, which allows for real combat and training scenarios for armed forces fighting anti-institutional groups. The CIA tends to use diplomats and consular employees as informants and/or agents, as well as military attachés and representatives of the Attorney General of Mexico (PGR), federal prosecutors and Mexican embassies in the United States and around the world. The same occurs with intelligence agents and members of the armed forces. Many actions undertaken against Mexican criminals as part of the war on drug trafficking have been carried out by American soldiers or paramilitaries, which contradicts the Mexican government's official story.[22]

The CIA has played a decisive role in Mexico through the criminal group of greatest paramilitary efficacy in strategic, logistical, tactical and operational terms: the Zetas, whose leaders received military training from the U.S. government as the elite soldiers of Mexico's Special Forces Airmobile Group (GAFES) and Guatemala's Kaibiles. CIA operations involving drug trafficking have previously been carried out in Vietnam, Nicaragua and Afghanistan.[23] The U.S. war machine would thus be a decisive factor in the upsurge of violence seen in Mexico in recent years, which has occurred in an international context marked by the threat of terrorism and the emergent geopolitics of the United States following September 11, 2001.

These activities follow two U.S. government directives. The first, from 1954, establishes that covert operations are the responsibility of the CIA and are to be planned and carried out in accordance with the military and diplomatic policies of the United States.[24] In the second, from 2002, the U.S. government's national security strategy no longer recognizes the principle of state sovereignty, which dates back to the Peace of Westphalia in 1648.[25]

And so the concept of sovereignty, one of Mexico's constitutional principles, has been dismantled under the ideology of integration and bilateral cooperation. In reality, the United States seeks to appropriate Mexico's natural, energy and human resources in order to strengthen its own geopolitical interests, offering in exchange the financing, advising and security needed for this appropriative process.

In the midst of political amnesia and omission, five cases have converged:

1. In 2008, the Mexican press reported that a private airplane with the tailnumber N987SA, used by the CIA for clandestine flights carrying alleged terrorists to the Guantánamo military base, crashed in Mérida in September 2007 with close to four tons of cocaine from the Sinaloa/Pacific Cartel aboard. The plane had been acquired for two million dollars in cash via transactions carried out through the Puebla Currency Exchange.[26] This information has been confirmed by two official sources: the DEA and the PGR.

It has also been reported that the Puebla Currency Exchange was being investigated by both Mexican and U.S. authorities for its alleged role in a financial network used by the Sinaloa/Pacific Cartel to launder drug money and even purchase airplanes used for transporting drugs.[27]

2. In 2010, as part of Colombia's Operation Fronteras, 21 people were arrested for their ties to the Puebla Currency Exchange's money laundering operations. The commander of the operation was the national police chief. Apart from his work for

the Colombian government, he has been domestically accused of working as an informant for U.S. intelligence agencies and protecting drug traffickers; his brother was found guilty of drug trafficking in Germany in 2006.[28] In 2012, the Mexican government announced that he had been hired as a security consultant; his relationships with criminals and U.S. intelligence agencies were denied and the case of his brother was overlooked.[29]

3. The role of the Puebla Currency Exchange in money laundering operations reappeared in a 2012 report by the U.S. Senate's Permanent Subcommittee on Investigations[30] that addresses the tolerance of money laundering by HSBC, along with similar operations by Monex, Sigue Corporation and Wachovia Bank.

This report describes many activities connected to money laundering. And it addresses the case of the Chinese-Mexican pharmaceutical executive who was found to be keeping $205 million in cash at his Mexico City residence, which was then seized by Mexican authorities.[31]

4. In U.S. custody while waiting to be extradited to Mexico, this businessman revealed that he had been threatened into holding the money by powerful individuals linked to the National Action Party (PAN) and Institutional Revolutionary Party (PRI).[32]

As was learned following his arrest, he had received preferential treatment when opening a pharmaceutical plant in Mexico State.[33] Though his operations were closely followed by the authorities in Mexico and the United States, he was able to import chemicals between 2001 and 2006, a period in which the director of the Federal Commission for the Protection against Sanitary Risk, the agency that grants permits for such activities, was a PRI operative.

To date, the PGR has revealed nothing on its investigations into the alleged responsibility of these government functionaries. Those arrested in connection to the seized money—his relatives, for example—have all been released.[34] The authorities were unable to prove any of the charges.

5. WikiLeaks has revealed that, with the assistance of the Swiss banker Julius Baer, a Mexican general was able to invest several million dollars in the Symac Trust between 1990 and 1998.[35] The following year, a Mexican government functionary who also served as an informant for the Federal Bureau of Investigation (FBI) offered evidence against this officer to Mexican and U.S. authorities. In 2000, the general was arrested and accused of aiding the Juárez Cartel. Two years later, he was sentenced to fifteen years in prison. He was exonerated in 2007 and his rank was restored to

him the following year. A CIA asset, a veteran of the Dirty War and a government consultant, the general was assassinated in Mexico City in 2012. Nothing more was ever heard about his millions.

A definition of geopolitics becomes necessary: a science that aims to base domestic or foreign policy on the systematic study of geographic, economic, racial, cultural and religious factors in light of the interests of a global power structure that converges with organized crime. What do we speak of when we speak of Mexico and its contemporary reality? As Hans Kelsen teaches us, there is no contradiction between experience and logic.[36]

The breakup of the old map of Mexico and the reconfiguration of its territory has involved the country's relentless militarization and paramilitarization, which includes community "self-defense" groups that often maintain ties to organized crime. A process connected to the new global context.

The Mexican government has denied the existence of paramilitary groups fighting criminals. This denial was made in Ciudad Juárez in 2011 during an announcement that the city's murder rate had fallen as a result of the government's crime-fighting strategy. And it was a response to a fact: a paramilitary group known as Los Matazetas had announced its presence in the Gulf Coast state of Veracruz.[37]

The rise of paramilitarism is not just a fact, but is also an informal consequence of the Mérida Initiative, whose precedent can be found in Plan Colombia.[38] The dynamics of the war on drug trafficking, as sponsored by the United States, allow for three possibilities, as can be seen in the historical record: the participation of domestic military and police forces, the intervention of U.S. agents and military personnel in covert operations and the presence of paramilitary groups.

The momentary reduction of violence in Ciudad Juárez is due to the paramilitary factor as much as it is to the military and police presence. Many powerful businessmen along the border have employed paramilitaries to protect their lives and properties.[39]

In its hurry to legitimize itself, the Mexican government has ignored the thousands of deaths and the social disintegration seen in the border city as a result of the war on drug trafficking, just as it has passed over the disappearances of young women. The government has also committed a very serious offense: it has refused to respond to the ruling of the Inter-American Court of Human Rights on the case of the women murdered in Ciudad Juárez's Campo Algodonero in 2001.[40] The government's defiance of the continent's highest court only adds to its contempt for the rule of law and its proclivity for authoritarian solutions, based around "special" considerations, to the problem of anti-institutional violence.[41] The "state of exception" and its use by democratic governments has become a dominant theme in ultracontemporary politics.[42]

In recent years, the Mexican government has boasted that it "neither murders nor represses."[43] This declaration is insistently made while dozens of legal reforms are being proposed that would expand the repressive powers of the state, many of which have already been put into practice despite their violation of constitutional rights and principles.[44] There are reports of thousands of human rights violations committed by police officers and soldiers. This problem has attracted the attention of the United Nations.[45] The official perspective is remarkable in its lack of a broader perspective on the effects of government actions, on the growing number of victims (who are offered charity, demagogy or bureaucratic solutions that only simulate a proper response) and on the rise of a police state and a paramilitarized society. A society that has seen its problems multiply due to a disastrous strategy in the fight against crime and instability, undertaken without assessing or modeling its risks.[46] Its failure has only strengthened the war machine and the geopolitical interests of the United States.

In this geopolitical environment, another important episode occurred in which the U.S.

government revealed an alleged plot to attack the United States that involved both Islamic fundamentalists and Mexican drug traffickers. There is an imperative to legally equate the latter with terrorists. Out of deference to this need, the Mexican government has proposed legislative reforms on the matter, while senators and bureaucrats in the United States push for drug traffickers to be considered terrorists.[47] In 2012, a group of alleged terrorists from the Lebanese Islamist organization Hezbollah were arrested in Mexico.[48] Yet another sign of the logic of war and violence imposed by U.S. intelligence agencies.

The goal is to increase the instability of Mexico in order to impose a "strong" state and to promote Mexico's role as the gendarme of the region to the south of the United States, which includes Central America and the Caribbean. The country to the north needs Mexico to provide the world's cheapest manual labor[49] for its maquiladoras: the majority of its exports are for the U.S. market and millions of Mexicans have gone there to work. Chaos, a crumbling educational system and the imposition of barbarism (arms, drugs, violence, mass exploitation) have become profitable under the asymmetrical geometry between Mexico and its neighbors to the north. Illegality is a major global business. The U.S. patronizes it, using its war machine as an economic platform: a shadowy scheme.

2

YEARS OF LEAD

In 2007, the Mexican government decided to launch a war on drug trafficking.[1] When this issue is analyzed, there's almost no mention of the role of the U.S. or of Mexico's institutional complicity in the rising violence and increasing prominence of the country's drug traffickers.

The conventional defense of the Mexican government reduces the matter to one of supply and demand: the U.S. shares responsibility for Mexico's problems due to its high levels of drug consumption and its indiscriminate sale of high-caliber weaponry to criminals. It is also said that past administrations have been inefficient and negligent in the fight against organized crime. Nothing is said of U.S. geopolitical interests that threaten the nation-state in Mexico and elsewhere.

Stratfor, for instance, is a think tank that advances the interests of the Pentagon, the arms industry and, sometimes, the State Department and other U.S. government agencies. It is considered to be something of an unofficial CIA. In general, its reports reflect the ideas and conceptual shifts of U.S. national security institutions.

In a 2012 Stratfor report on drug trafficking in Mexico, two important points can be discerned: 1) the seizure of fifteen tons of methamphetamines in Guadalajara, Jalisco, which would indicate that Mexican drug traffickers have undergone a "major change" in their criminal activities by transforming themselves from intermediaries to the controllers of a profitable, independent market; and 2) that Mexican drug traffickers are not cartels, as cartels are defined by their use of commercial agreements to stabilize prices, and it would therefore be more accurate to refer to them by using the label proposed by the DEA: Transnational Criminal Organizations (TCOs).[2]

These two points, rather than observing provable facts, develop a strategic analysis that represents a change in focus, conceptual-operational staging and terminology in order to better serve the transformations in U.S. geopolitical strategy that will be seen in the near future.

In terms of the first point, we can state that reality contradicts Stratfor's allegations: Mexican drug traffickers have been growing marijuana and opium poppies for several decades now. And they've been doing so on a large scale. Of course, they have also served as intermediaries for South

American cocaine being transported elsewhere. Their experience and organizational capacity have led them to adapt their activities to changing circumstances and market demand (which also includes other criminal industries besides drug trafficking). For them, methamphetamine production is far from being a "major change": it's simply yet another adaptation to their changing context, not to mention one that goes back fifteen years.

This first point should instead be read as a reconceptualization of Mexican drug traffickers—whose internal business structures have been systematic and effective throughout their history—with the goal of situating them on a higher threat level, as specified by the second point: by labelling them as "transnational criminal organizations," they will consequently be seen not as mere cartels operating in a particular country or territory but as "terrorists," as stateless enemies. This distinction is crucial. In Colombia, this explanatory model has been in use since 2003 and has helped to consolidate the militarization of society.

The suspicion of terrorism radicalizes and loosens the construction of the image of the enemy, which allows for the indiscriminate use of armed violence in the name of internal security, as well as the unprovoked declaration of war against foreign states, the normalization and institutionalization of states of exception and, lastly, the use of extralegal measures not just in international relations and against enemy terrorists, but also within the state itself, as well as in its relations with foreign democracies.[3] Constitutional principles become subjected to executive orders.

The Stratfor report conceals one factor that is of immediate relevance whenever methamphetamine is analyzed in the context of the global drug trade: the influence of Southeast Asia (Thailand, Laos) and the Chinese Triads, as well as the geopolitical interests of the People's Republic of China. The Chinese-Mexican connection is the background that Stratfor avoids, though it can be seen in China's penetration of Mexican territory through the purchase of land and property along the border, where real estate values have fallen due to crime.[4]

In the emerging global order, TCOs must be examined as a phenomenon that is inseparable from that of the multinational armed forces that fight them, coordinated by the United States.

An increasingly hardline U.S. position on drug policy is on Mexico's horizon. And violence continues to escalate, to the bewilderment of the authorities, who no longer allude to this problem in terms of a war on drug trafficking, as they did just months beforehand, but in terms of a war between drug traffickers.

The changing focus of the official story is significant: up until 2012, the Mexican government emphasized that the country's violence had little to do with its strategy in the fight against organized crime, but was instead a product of the violence of the criminals themselves. The authorities also explained, however, that the violent reaction of certain criminal groups to their repressive operations—such as the eradication of crops, the seizure of their assets and the arrest of their leaders—proved the wisdom of their strategy. This paradoxical vacillation between opposing points of view demonstrated the disarray of the government, which, so as not to completely relinquish power, conducted limited tactical operations consisting of overdue and inefficient patrols through conflict zones, deploying the armed forces (army, navy and federal police) throughout the towns of the Gulf Coast and northern and central-western Mexico. Likewise, each time a drug lord fell, the story was always inconsistent.[5]

The Mexican government proudly proclaims that it has declared a war on all criminal groups without exception, with constant attacks on their leaders, but this has only led to the increase in violence seen in Mexico between 2007 and 2012. The geographical distribution of this violence speaks to something much more complex than the official story of crime rates, localized and finite, of little importance. The problem of violence and insecurity in Mexico has reached alarming dimensions. In 2012, it was connected to the rivalry between two major cartels—the Sinaloa/Pacific Cartel and the Zetas—as well as their respective allies.

At the beginning of 2013, the government put forward a plan to focus the fight against organized crime and bring down the country's homicide, kidnapping and extortion rates. This plan included planning guidelines, crime prevention measures, human rights safeguards and institutional coordination and transformations, in which the Interior Secretariat would take responsibility for public safety through a "national gendarmerie" under its command that would increase the government's control over the country's borders and other strategic regions with the support of five regional police training centers and a National Intelligence Center that would complement the Binational Intelligence Office.[6] This new anti-crime strategy maintains the role of the army and the navy in police work, as in the previous stage of the war on drug trafficking: a warning of a change in our model of civilization. This strategy has two dimensions: 1) to meet Mexico's commitments under the Mérida Initiative, whose goal is to put a war machine (sponsored and directed by the U.S.) into operation south of its borders; and 2) to simulate a change away from the practices of the previous administration through the use of a "pacifist" discourse while continuing the inertia of its policies.

Mexican and U.S. analysts tend to observe the problem of violence in Mexico as if it occurred in a territory isolated from political and geopolitical tensions, in which violent phenomena can be analyzed from a limited criminological perspective that presents contemporary reality as a straightforward struggle between the government and organized crime. And they occasionally utilize data on the market and the underground economy to round out their analytical position. The more refined their explanatory models or their handling of the data, the more they overlook the historical context and the corruption of Mexico's institutions, which are subject as never before in their history to a power struggle involving both domestic and foreign interests.

Mexico's instability is connected to a factor that is only infrequently mentioned by analysts: the manipulation of criminal organizations by the Pentagon, acting through the CIA. This occurs as the DEA breaks up the old ties between the Mexican Army and the Juárez Cartel, as well as its successor, the Sinaloa/Pacific Cartel.

The 2012 arrests of three Mexican generals, as demanded by the DEA and carried out by the PGR, occurred in this political and geopolitical context, which implies readjustments within the armed forces.[7] They were released the following year due to lack of evidence regarding their alleged organized crime ties.

The operational presence of the CIA and other security agencies in Mexico is as undeniable as the Mexican government's relinquishment of national sovereignty.

In 2006, the Mexican government found itself overwhelmed by its obligation to comply with the Security and Prosperity Partnership of North America, which it had signed in 2005.

The primary consequence of this agreement was the creation of the Mérida Initiative in 2008, which culminated in 2010 and whose continuation has been negotiated with the U.S. Congress since 2012. Financially, it includes 250 million pesos for the Mexican government per year, to be spent on crime prevention, penal and security reforms, human rights safeguards, border security and the professionalization of federal, state and municipal police forces.[8]

Mexico's institutional degradation has not left its intelligence services untouched. They were dismantled years ago and reduced to the status of just another government bureaucracy, open to corruption, while espionage groups answering to particular politicians carried out illegal investigations.[9]

On the pretext of implementing the Mérida Initiative, the U.S. government has taken over operational intelligence tasks in Mexico, acting above the country's own armed forces and intervening in the war on drug trafficking in defense of U.S. national security interests.

The U.S. security agencies operating in Mexico not only oversee the implementation of the Mérida Initiative, but also manipulate Mexican drug traffickers in support of their geopolitical interests, as they have done at other times in their history. Both the DEA and CIA have operated in this manner.[10]

The joint actions undertaken by these agencies with regard to Mexican drug trafficking cartels and organizations have occurred in three phases: 1) weakening or attacking some groups (the Beltrán Leyvas and the Gulf Cartel) to strengthen others (the Sinaloa/Pacific Cartel and the Zetas); 2) disbanding (or eliminating) the strategic contacts of older operatives and informants (ex-Juárez Cartel, ex-Federation) with the DEA and CIA;[11] 3) channeling the transition of older cartel operatives towards the establishment of new urban and suburban criminal groups of a paramilitary nature (the Knights Templar, the Legionnaires), whose control of markets, routes and territories is based on the corruption of the police and government functionaries (for example, in Acapulco, along the Pacific coast or in central Mexico). The struggle of "all against all"[12] produced the hegemony of the Sinaloa/Pacific Cartel and the Zetas as the pole of opposition to the

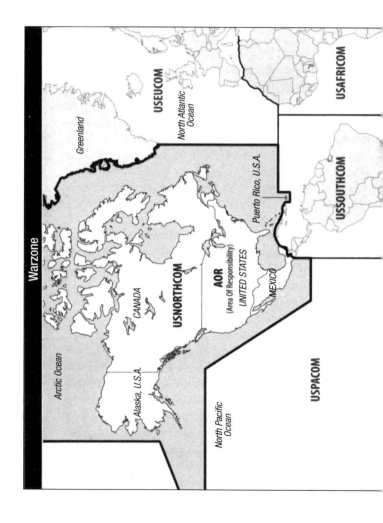

Northern Command, personified by Mexico's armed forces and police, as well as by the U.S. soldiers and special agents operating in Mexico.

The strategy employed indicates that, without counter-institutional force, it would be impossible to consolidate the restructuring of Mexico's armed forces, bringing them up to the military, immigration, border, maritime, port, airport and information security standards of NORTHCOM, which Mexico joined in 2002 alongside Canada and the United States. The complement of this geopolitically assimilationist policy resides in a criminal justice reform whose core is the implementation of the adversarial justice process, commonly known as oral trials, in the Mexican judicial system.[13]

The U.S. intelligence office created under the Mérida Initiative employs dozens of former police officers and government officials who follow the orders of a variety of U.S. security agencies.[14]

The lesson learned from all this is of the utmost importance for Mexico, Central America and the Caribbean, representing not just the loss of national sovereignty through policies that sweep aside constitutional principles on arguments of integration and cooperation, but also that politicians have willingly chosen to become nothing more than the representatives of the geopolitical interests of the United States. The destruction of their country is unimportant: they are the servants on call in

America's backyard. The Mexican government, for example, has authorized the construction of U.S. military bases in its territory.[15]

In 2012, the Mexican government announced that the country's homicide rate had fallen, an announcement that was intended to show the world that the war on drug trafficking had provided satisfactory results. The facts indicate the contrary.

According to the National Public Security Council, the second half of 2011 and the first half of 2012 saw the first decline in the homicide rate since 2007, the year in which the government launched its strategy of armed confrontation, with a 7% decline in the number of murders.

Non-governmental organizations immediately contested the significance of this reported decline, which, according to the official figures themselves, is actually only 4.32%. The government's "hard data" turned out to be false. This manipulation of information is a recurrent phenomenon with the Mexican government, no matter which party is in power. Between 2007 and 2012, there were more than 60,000 murders (others estimate up to 120,000 murders) and criminal violence led to more than 7,000 deaths in the first half of 2012, or 10% more than in the six preceding months.[16] The official fictions shrivel under the light of independent studies.

The Mexican government contemplates its collapse: not only has it failed to keep its primary promise ("the government of jobs"), but the geopolitical strategy of the United States has impelled it to fight drug trafficking, reform its judicial system and improve public safety, tasks it undertook with more brute force than intelligence. The results are clear: a country devastated by violence, with insecurity the rule over almost all its territory.

By using the army, navy and air force for police work, the government has threatened the substance of constitutional principles, as the Supreme Court has recently argued.[17] Unfortunately, politicians have preferred to cling to a formalist notion of what they understand as legality instead of respecting the constitutional rule of law.

The Mexican government tried to convince the army, navy and air force to accept a special operation by U.S. forces in its territory, resembling the one that took out Osama bin Laden, to apprehend or kill the drug trafficker Joaquín *El Chapo* Guzmán.[18] Mexico's armed forces refused: accepting such an operation would represent a violation of the country's sovereignty and its constitutional principles. Mexican marine commandos, coordinated by the U.S., were eventually able to arrest Guzmán in 2014, when he gave himself up without offering any resistance.

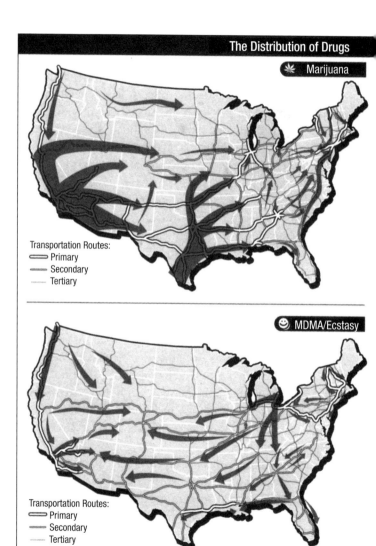

The Distribution of Drugs

Marijuana

Transportation Routes:
— Primary
— Secondary
— Tertiary

MDMA/Ecstasy

Transportation Routes:
— Primary
— Secondary
— Tertiary

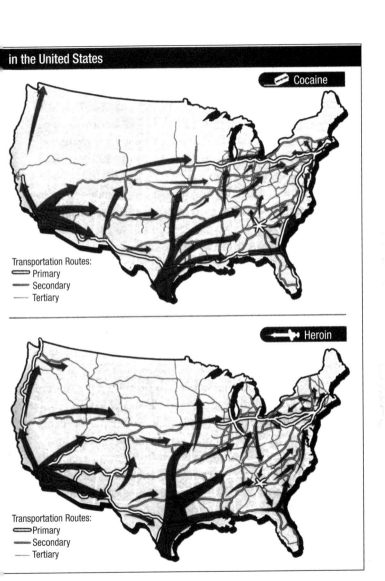

Cocaine

Transportation Routes:
⬭ Primary
— Secondary
— Tertiary

Heroin

Transportation Routes:
⬭ Primary
— Secondary
— Tertiary

In 2012, a pair of CIA agents were ambushed near Mexico City. They were fired upon by alleged criminals, supported by federal police officers (the official story states that these officers were "investigating a kidnapping"). The two Americans, who were accompanied by a naval officer, managed to escape in an armored car.[19]

The authorities of both of the countries implicated in this incident have provided scant information. The stories that circulated afterwards contradicted each other on three key points: 1) the presence of armed agents of the U.S. government in Mexican territory, 2) the reason why federal police officers participated in the assault on the agents, 3) the role of the naval officer who accompanied the CIA agents.

The shootout with the CIA agents occurred in a municipality located on the border between Mexico City, Mexico State and Morelos, lying along a corridor for criminal operations between Mexico's capital and the Pacific, particularly the port of Acapulco. This zone has been the site of a struggle that goes back years between different criminal organizations, particularly the Zetas, the Sinaloa/Pacific Cartel and their offshoot: the Beltrán Leyvas, who have been the primary target for Mexico and the United States since 2008 because of their high level of efficacy in both countries. In the end, the FBI concluded that there had been a direct attack on U.S. agents ordered by the Beltrán Leyvas. Mexican authorities explained that the three federal agents who participated in the attack did so by mistake during their investigation of a kidnapping.

This incident marked a breaking point for the Mérida Initiative. The institution with which the Americans have worked most closely has been the Navy Secretariat (SEMAR).

The geopolitical posture of the U.S. government regarding the trafficking of drugs from Mexico to the United States has three aspects: 1) national security (and the threat of terrorism, given the hypothesis of a possible connection between international criminal organizations and Middle Eastern fundamentalist groups), 2) control of the drug market (distribution and consumption) in the United States and along the border with Mexico, and 3) the manipulation of Mexican drug cartels in the configuration of a new military-police action map with respect to Central America and the Caribbean, which has imposed social instability on Mexico through drug violence and the consequent strengthening of the military-police state.

One interpretation of the problem of U.S. intelligence agents in Mexico has been the allegation that the authorization of the executive branch is enough to sidestep any issues of national sovereignty, which implies that the authority of the president or the armed forces is above that of the constitution. Unfortunately, due to these attitudes that threaten constitutional principles, Mexico has blindly launched a war whose inertia will prolong its violence far into the future.

In 2012, a U.S. State Department employee was freed who had worked in years past as an assistant to a high-ranking Mexican bureaucrat who was imprisoned in 2008 under Mexico's Operation Limpieza, which targeted corrupt PGR employees and their connections with the Beltrán Leyvas. He was exonerated in 2013. If this double agent was involved in these events, then we can confirm that this operation was orchestrated, and not simply instigated, by the U.S. government.[20]

The revelation of CIA activities in Mexico and the geopolitical interests of the United States in Mexican criminal organizations and drug cartels has also uncovered the internal struggle for control of the Defense Secretariat.[21]

The U.S. government has publicly and privately expressed its lack of confidence in this particular branch of Mexico's armed forces, preferring instead to work with the Navy Secretariat, which it considers to be less corrupt, as can be seen in a cable from the United States government announcing a collaboration and confidentiality agreement to be renewed each year by both countries.

The cable states: "It is our understanding that no further Mexican government approval is necessary for this agreement to enter into force in Mexico once signed, beyond the approval already granted by [the Foreign Relations Secretariat]." The purpose of this agreement is to enable a "smoother and swifter exchange of such information with SEMAR, especially between military counterparts," and to regulate the exchange of classified national security information between both parties, which may be categorized as "confidential," "secret" and "top secret."[22]

It is significant that the new military doctrines use terminology that alludes to smoothness, flexibility and fluidity,[23] as is their emphasis on having effective information strategies. This suggests the challenge of counteracting networks of combative or insurrectionary agents—whether they be terrorists, guerrillas, drug cartels, gangs or nonviolent social activists—through the use of analogous networks.[24]

Mexico's 2012 transition of power indicates the continuity of a political orthodoxy that goes back three decades: the megaplan of the absorption of Mexico by the United States, as seen in the North American Free Trade Agreement (NAFTA) in the last decade of the 20th century, as well as in the Security and Prosperity Partnership of North America (SPP) in the first decade of the 21st.[25]

The logic of war's immediate effect on Mexico has not only been a modification of the map of the country's interior, but also that of its cities. By the beginning of the second decade of the 21st century, Mexico's cities were characterized by their high rates of violent crimes, particularly homicide. In statistical terms, five Mexican cities were among the world's ten most violent urban areas (Ciudad Juárez, Acapulco, Torreón, Chihuahua, Durango). And this was part of a larger problem of continental scope: America, particularly Latin America, was home to 45 of the world's 50 most violent cities. Ciudad Juárez was considered the world's second most violent city after San Pedro Sula in Honduras.[26]

The process of degradation over the past ten years has been clear. For example: Monterrey, the capital of Nuevo León in the north of the country, near the U.S. border, was a pole of industrial development throughout the 20th century that wielded economic influence both domestically and internationally. Like many Mexican cities, it is characterized by its social contrasts: the concentration of wealth in a small number of families, with inequality and poverty for the majority.[27] The third most important city in the country, surrounded by mountains and hills.

Widespread drug consumption led to rising violence: between 1991 and 2005, drug use among young people doubled. Together with stricter

Criminal Organizations

Drug cartels,
*criminal organizations with an
international reach (Gulf Cartel,
Sinaloa/Pacific Cartel, the Zetas)
and their protective matrix*

Gangs

The Armed Forces

The war against the
armed forces

The Population

The population
*(and human reserve
of potential victims)*

customs controls along the U.S. border—which stimulated Mexico's domestic drug supply—the government's war on drug trafficking, the struggle among criminal groups and the economic crisis, the demand for drugs had an influence on rising rates of domestic violence, burglary, robbery and auto theft.

In 2010, Nuevo León went from being one of the safest states in the country to one of its three most dangerous: extortion, robbery, burglary, kidnapping, land theft and human trafficking proliferated, creating an atmosphere of violence and a growing number of victims. The long-term effect has been a crisis of governability, institutional incompetence and corruption, falling rates of investment, changes in social patterns, rising spending on security, shuttered businesses, exile.

The destructuring of social space has affected the community cartography, which has seen its spatial and temporal patterns reduced, just as personal circulation routes have been altered. And a new order/disorder has arisen in the urban and suburban environment, above all thanks to the increase in gang activity and its effect on the crime rate, which brings together three dimensions: that of drug cartels (the Gulf Cartel, the Sinaloa/Pacific Cartel, the Zetas) and their protective matrix, that of the population (and the human reserve of potential victims) and that of the war against the armed forces.[28]

Due to the differences between convergent actors, this three-dimensionality makes violence both repeated and localized in changing zones of friction under overlapping local jurisdictions (drug trafficking routes, temporary delimitations, points of sale, etc.). Unlike other cities that have seen the rise of supergangs, like Los Aztecas of Ciudad Juárez, Monterrey has smaller gangs and common criminals with territory downtown and in the north (Colonia Valle Santa Lucía), in the north-west (Topo Chico), in the northeast (Escobedo), San Nicolás de los Garza, downtown Apodaca, the western edge of Apodaca, downtown Guadalupe, southern Monterrey (Cerro de la Campana) and Juárez-Cadereyta Jiménez. The localization of these criminal *focos*, no matter how circumscribed they may seem, nevertheless implies elasticity and expansionism due to the ties of these gangs to drug cartels. Their strength comes from their plunder of the civilian population, which allows them to accumulate extraordinary monetary, material and human resources through extortion, kidnapping, robbery, identity theft, coercion, etc. The meaning of private property and its established boundaries have been inverted, revolving around or alternating with criminal disorder.

The corruption of the authorities makes it impossible for citizens to restore the normality they once knew in public and private. The trends that have marked the war on drug trafficking indicate that these gangs will mutate into super-gangs with the support of telecommunications technology: mobile phones, the Internet, social media.[29] This emergent or transmediatic spatiality interacts with conventional space, allowing gangs to amplify their criminal activities and increase the flexibility of the territory they dominate, as well as that of ordinary citizens. Their ties to transnational drug cartels will be decisive in building connections with corrupt authorities.

In Acapulco, Guerrero, on the southern Pacific coast, two gangs predominate: La Barredora and the Independent Cartel of Acapulco, both based in the outskirts of the city. The territory of Acapulco consists of the eponymous bay, the surrounding mountains and the settlements stretching along the coast in both directions as well as inland, towards the mountains. In their struggle over this territory, criminals invade important thoroughfares: the Maxitunnel on Highway 95, the downtown historic district, the Y (where Highway 200 intersects 95), the northwestern periphery, the eastside.[30]

An important domestic and international tourist destination, Acapulco is being strangled by the coercive activities of criminal groups that operate not just in the suburbs, but in the heart of the city and throughout the metropolitan area. The bay and its tourism and entertainment services have become a bottleneck of extreme danger. The fight against crime only ever has a temporary impact as the authorities try to reduce violence without attacking the roots of criminal enterprises. The result is an alegal environment whose flexible space puts pressure on laws and regulations and reformulates social customs. The perimeter of the bay, where the tourism infrastructure and services are located, delineates a criminal reserve.

The war against drug trafficking in Mexico began with the "pilot project" of Ciudad Juárez, which converted this border city into an even more dangerous and desolate place than it already was in the previous decade: abandoned homes, shuttered businesses, orphaned children, 200,000 families living in exile. In these years, the Mexican Army has mobilized an average of 48,000 soldiers across the country each month to fight drug cartels, carrying out close to 200,000 patrols. Despite this military campaign, organized crime has strengthened its position, both inside and outside the country's borders.[31]

In Ciudad Juárez, the Mexican government has implemented three different plans, accompanied by other actions, to try and establish its control. Each failure has multiplied the problems of a territory ravaged by organized crime, institutional corruption and an absent government.

In the spring of 2008, a joint operation, which would later be known as Operation Coordinada, was launched in the state of Chihuahua. Soldiers and federal police officers took over local security responsibilities, installing ten joint operations bases and 46 mobile checkpoints. They had at their disposal 180 vehicles and 13 "molecular detection" units for drugs, explosives, weapons and money, as well as three C-130 Hercules military transport aircraft and one Boeing 727/110 airplane on loan from the Mexican Air Force. At first, 2,500 soldiers were deployed; the next year there would be 7,000, plus 2,000 federal police officers.

Soldiers and federal police officers occupied different points of the city and carried out patrols and other tactical operations. The city was so threatened that residents rejected their presence: reports of the abuses of the armed forces piled up in the archives of domestic and international human rights organizations.[32] The army would later be pushed aside in favor of the federal police at the request of the United States. Aside from a few privileged areas, urban life occurs in a climate of war and the struggle for collective survival.

One example of the limitless violence of the criminal organizations fighting for control of the city can be seen in a series of events that occurred in 2010: a commando unit attacked dozens of young people at a party. Sixteen people were killed.

Weeks later, a similar attack occurred at another party. One person died and seven were wounded. These types of attacks on young people in private spaces were repeated over the course of the year. In 2010, Ciudad Juárez even saw the murder of a U.S. Embassy employee and a car bombing. And the federal police fired on a group of young people who were protesting the city's violence.

The decline of the Juárez Cartel and the rise of the Pacific Cartel as the strongest organization along the border has reconfigured this territory, which is also claimed by the Zetas. The area's supergangs include Los Aztecas, Los Artistas Asesinos, Los Mexicles, La Mara Salvatrucha, the Mexican Mafia and Barrio 18—together, it's estimated that they have a total of 20,000 members—and around them, smaller groups like Barrio 22, Barrio Noveno and Pandilla 357 prosper.[33]

The metropolitan area is divided from north to south and from east to west, with the areas caught in the middle subjected to a daily struggle under the growing domination of the Sinaloa/Pacific Cartel. Homicides are on the rise in the poorest neighborhoods. In the tourist/business district, as well as in the industrial parks run by transnational corporations, there is a level of security that is non-existent in poor neighborhoods. A city of great fluidity in terms of private transportation and interpersonal communication, its territory is

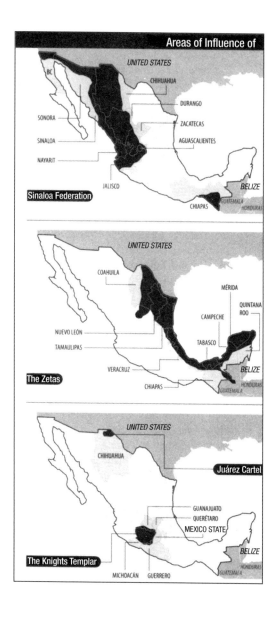

Areas of Influence of

UNITED STATES

BC

CHIHUAHUA

DURANGO

SONORA

ZACATECAS

SINALOA

AGUASCALIENTES

NAYARIT

JALISCO

BELIZE

GUATEMALA

CHIAPAS

HONDURAS

Sinaloa Federation

UNITED STATES

COAHUILA

MÉRIDA

QUINTANA
ROO

NUEVO LEÓN

CAMPECHE

TAMAULIPAS

TABASCO

VERACRUZ

BELIZE

CHIAPAS

HONDURAS

GUATEMALA

The Zetas

UNITED STATES

CHIHUAHUA

Juárez Cartel

GUANAJUATO

QUERÉTARO

MEXICO STATE

BELIZE

The Knights Templar

MICHOACÁN

GUERRERO

HONDURAS

GUATEMALA

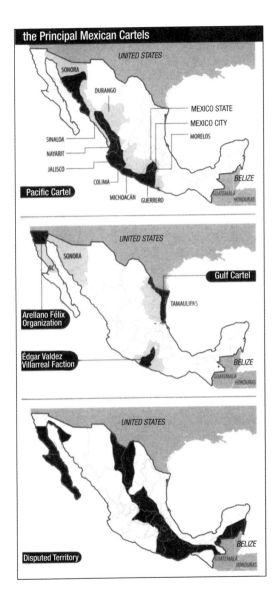

the Principal Mexican Cartels

Pacific Cartel

UNITED STATES
SONORA
DURANGO
MEXICO STATE
MEXICO CITY
MORELOS
SINALOA
NAYARIT
JALISCO
COLIMA
MICHOACÁN   GUERRERO
BELIZE
GUATEMALA
HONDURAS

UNITED STATES
SONORA
BC
Gulf Cartel
TAMAULIPAS
Arellano Félix Organization
Édgar Valdez Villarreal Faction
BELIZE
GUATEMALA
HONDURAS

UNITED STATES
Disputed Territory
BELIZE
GUATEMALA
HONDURAS

valuable as a strategic border crossing for smuggling drugs into the United States, a circumstance that has molded its collective life through the daily combat between criminal groups and the armed forces, which goes back years.

In Guadalajara, the influence of the Sinaloa/Pacific Cartel and the Zetas has led to the rise of two smaller, regional groups: the Jalisco New Generation Cartel and El Milenio, which have both evolved from street gangs.[34] Guadalajara is located in a valley and borders the municipalities of Zapopan and Ixtlahuacán del Río to the north, Tonalá and Zapotlanejo to the east, Tlaquepaque to the south and Zapopan to the west. With slightly less than five million residents, it is the country's second most important city. Its rising homicide rate is linked to the struggle among criminal groups for control of its territory.

In 2012, violence rose sharply in central Mexico, which includes the states of Querétaro, Michoacán, Guanajuato and Jalisco, where the Sinaloa/Pacific Cartel, the Zetas, El Milenio, La Familia Michoacana and the Knights Templar control territories and transportation routes. Along with the northern and southern borders, the Pacific coast and the Gulf of Mexico, central Mexico is being configured as a determining vector of the future field of battle, in general through the strengthening of the armed forces and in particular through the consolidation of federal, state and municipal police forces.[35] As criminal groups have improved their organization, tactical resources, manpower and armaments, so have the armed forces (army, air force, navy and police) secured ever-increasing budgets: between 2000 and 2006, their budget was increased by nearly 25%, and between 2007 and 2013, the budgetary increase was 97%, money that was spent on purchasing tactical vehicles, surveillance aircraft and patrol ships, as well as rescue and combat helicopters: the fourth highest military budget in Latin America.[36] The logic of war has been set in motion.

In Michoacán, the Knights Templar, a criminal organization founded in 2011 following a split from La Familia Michoacana, is being contained by "community self-defense" groups or paramilitaries that claim to oppose them and other criminal groups.

Located in the west of the country along the Pacific coast, Michoacán is a strategic state because of its natural resources and economic activities, which include significant levels of drug production and trafficking (marijuana, poppies/heroin, South American cocaine, metamphetamine) by different cartels and criminal groups. The international scope of these activities has made Michoacán into a field of battle and geopolitical interests.

The Mexican government recognizes that the Knights Templar control the export of millions of tons of iron to China each year. Since 2004, the U.S. government has been warning of the danger that Al Qaeda-affiliated terrorists could enter Mexico via Michoacán, aided by local drug traffickers, and then cross the northern border.

Due to the institutional crisis throughout the country, but particularly in Michoacán, society lives under the rule of crime instead of the rule of law. The federal government decided to confront this problem by launching a strategy with two initial phases: 1) taking direct control of the conflict zone; 2) creating conditions for the institutionalization of self-defense groups. And it announced a recovery plan for Michoacán that would involve economic stimuli, policing and aid, which were administered through a special commissioner whose powers were greater than those of the state's constituted powers.

The federal government's actions in Michoacán worsened the state's level of repression, the groundwork for which had been laid by the previous administration, and broadened the use of states of exception to confront emergencies in which the enemy is distinguished by the logic of asymmetric warfare. If some are imprisoned or eliminated, others will take their place. A low-intensity war with no end in sight.

In urban communities, which are dominant across the planet for the first time in human history, a cosmopolitan politics has taken root whose vision is both global and increasingly precise in its grasp of things and human beings, who tend to be seen as digital units integrated into networks and technological systems.[37] A model of control and surveillance merging corporate interests with those of the military, the necessary omniscient complement of the global order, which has generalized itself before the anxious eyes of ordinary citizens, whose lives are disturbed by the transcendence and fatality of becoming yet another statistic determined by superindividual powers.

This model is based on authoritarianism and the punitive impulse, imposing a model of social control that tends to delimit unequal social classes, fostering the potential for counterinsurgency in poor suburbs and the urban periphery. Under the idea of the comprehensive control and surveillance of urban spaces, citizens are the enemy of the military and the police.

States and societies in crisis that lose their monopoly on the use of force accept the everyday use of a variety of forms of repression and coercion. War centralizes itself in cities and a security economy emerges under the control of transnational corporations, dispossessing countries of their national sovereignty as part of the normalization of the Anglo-Saxon concept of the homeland, which was reformulated by the United States in the early years of the 21st century as the planetwide guarantee of its own national sovereignty.[38]

Under this strategy, which implicates the world's primary metropoles (New York, London, Beijing, Paris, Tokyo, Madrid, etc.), the Mexico City government has installed a system of surveillance cameras that reinscribe urban territory with a militarized omniscience. Thus it hopes to bring down the crime rate.[39]

The concept of the field of battle encompasses and penetrates everything, from the molecular scales of genetic engineering and nanotechnology to the sites, spaces and experiences of everyday urban life to the planetary spheres of tangible space and the global scope of immaterial cyberspace.[40]

The forecast for Mexico includes the normalization of violence at the community level, the strengthening of the repressive state and the implementation of the war machine as a consequence of the country's status as the backyard of the United States. In other countries, the strengthening of the military and the police has reformulated society. It is well known that the first casualty in war is the truth.[41] Instability and conflict tend to be very productive for certain economic and political powers: they dehumanize. An omen of the transhuman condition of the 21st century.

3

ANAMORPHOSIS OF THE VICTIM

For the legal system, the victim tends to be one of the actors present or convergent in an act of violence. Their existence is part of a legal-investigative narrative that resolves conflicts and assesses damages.[1] From a legal perspective, the victim forms part of an edifice (that of the law) with an equitable, hierarchical design implying balance, symbolically evoking the goddess Themis holding the scales of justice or a cornucopia, or perhaps the pyramid of law.[2] In these conceptions, the victim aspires to be seen and considered as a person who acquires corporeality in their spatial-temporal relationship with the sphere of law.

The victim is aware that they are outside a vast, labyrinthine edifice that is, nevertheless, nearby. And that they are defenseless, as in the Franz Kafka parable *Before the Law*:[3] a man from the country, the victim of some injustice, finds himself before the door to the law, whose doorkeeper denies him access and wastes his time in idle conversation and endless questions and answers. He grows desperate. The victim hears the doorkeeper say, "If you are so strongly tempted, try to get in without my permission. But note that I am powerful. And I am only the lowest doorkeeper. From hall to hall, keepers stand at every door, one more powerful than the other. And the sight of the third man is already more than even I can stand." Years go by and the victim grows old. His eyesight dimming and no longer able to raise his stiffening body, he still has one question that he has never yet put to the doorkeeper: "Everyone strives to attain the Law. How does it come about, then, that in all these years no one has come seeking admission but me?" The doorkeeper responds, "No one but you could gain admittance through this door, since this door was intended for you. I am now going to shut it." Faced with the impossibility of obtaining justice, the victim has only one certainty: that of gravitating around the law. They do not know if they will be heard and their very identity melds with that of others who share their fate. In the absence of justice, the victim's conformity tends to reduce them to a mere number, alongside others, in some official record.

The victim's journey forces us to remember that the only thing that can challenge the homogeneity promised and upheld by the law is their extreme experience of violence, the non-transferable specificity

Anamorphosis of the Victim

Faced with the impossibility of obtaining justice, the victim has only one certainty: that of gravitating around the law. They do not know if they will be heard and their very identity melds with that of others who share their fate.

Victim

Anamorphosis
The distortion of a person's everyday stability by a violent event.

This contrasts with the symmetry of the law and the institutions responsible for guaranteeing the rights of the victim through mechanisms, measures and procedures.

Victim

Between these realities lies the threshold at which politics is the axis or lynchpin of a permanent, virtual conflict: a wound, a crack, a rift that the institutions are unable to address, and so it opens ever wider and never closes. In the face of this rupture, the victim disassociates.

of their body, their understanding of the moment in which they became the target of a crime, an abuse, an atrocity. The distortion of a person's everyday stability by a violent event, which we will term the anamorphosis[4] of the victim, contrasts with the symmetry of the law and the institutions responsible for guaranteeing the rights of the victim through mechanisms, measures and procedures. It describes and alludes to the direct experience of harm, loss, danger, threats or other circumstances that threaten their human rights.

The gap between the event as experienced by the victim and the law that applies to the event reveals two opposed realities: the first is experienced as an anamorphosis—that is, an image, representation or memory that is deformed and confused, or steady and precise, depending on where or when it is evoked; the second tends to symmetry. Between these realities lies the threshold at which politics is the axis or lynchpin of a permanent, virtual conflict: a wound, a crack, a rift that the institutions are unable to address, and so it opens ever wider and never closes. In the face of this rupture, the victim disassociates. This disassociation takes them back to the original traumatic experience: their continuous attachment to the anamorphosis of the irrational, the a-rational, the terror and panic of reliving the unspeakable. Chaos without end.

The condition of the victim can only be overcome through a symbolic exchange with death. And even then, the victim reappears as an anamorphosis of their own memory: broken, deformed, overwritten with an incongruous representation of the familiar in which the personal has become distant, alien and unknown, their emotions overwhelmed by atrocity and cruelty at the hands of others. The world becomes an anamorphosis: a sinister design asserts itself. An oscillation between normality and anormality. And at the center of it all, the victim: their chronic experiences at the threshold of destruction.

The victim tends to appear as part of a legal investigation that confers an identity connecting their experiences at the limit between life and death to an institutional review process concerning the incident and its probable outcomes. Their experiences are made to fit into a chronological logic and subjected to an imperative to go ever further back (precedents) to explain the truth of what occurred. And though the victim is situated outside the legal order, their existence on Earth is subjected to the logic of the document, of legal investigations, in which human phenomena are reduced to letters (or perhaps numbers) that fill columns of penal records.

If, instead of understanding the victim as they appear in a chronological account that forms but one grain of sand in the great hourglass of shared existence, or as a marker of linear time, we understand them starting from their corporeality, their presence in a given space, their path through a three-dimensional environment—or four-dimensional, if we add the conceptual sphere—that is, their humanity in all its morphological, geographical and transgeographical aspects (the latter concerning telecommunications and its territory, Cyberia), the results would offer better information on the person and their transformation into a victim. By situating the victim in a space, an individual body emerges from the social body: a cultural topography, a critical spatial perspective. A cartography of the victims resituates the harm, the loss, the injury.

A body that is a person. A life that finds itself defenseless before the power that dominates and annihilates it: bare life.[5] To understand the anamorphosis of the victim, we must examine cases that clarify the influence of space and the new cartography of the field of battle on the civilians who endure it in a variety of places and circumstances.

Body/person of Adriana Ruiz:[6] a model and hostess in the city of Tijuana, the mother of a young boy and the provider for her family. She works in public relations. As part of her job, she promotes herself on social media: she publicizes her image and her professional experience. She has participated in beauty contests and appeared in advertisements. The company she works for belongs to a local power group. One Saturday, she is kidnapped outside her front door by a group of armed men. Her family reports the kidnapping. The media spreads the news. There's pressure on the authorities. Four days later, the police announce the discovery of the victim's body and the arrest of her murderers. The body of the girl is found half-buried in a garbage dump in the Altiplano neighborhood on the outskirts of the city. She has been decapitated. There are signs of torture: they've pulled out her toenails and cut off one toe from each foot. The accused confess: their crime boss ordered them to kidnap, interrogate, torture and decapitate the victim as a warning "to the others." Their criminal organization, which permeates the urban environment, believed that she was an informant, as she was accused of being by women close to the criminals. The police find the victim's phone in the possession of the murderers: they used its camera to record her decapitation. The authorities emphasize the connections between the victim and her victimizers. Her family denies these connections. The press denounces the haste with which the police arrested the murderers, as well as the many contradictions and lacunae of their official report. The police respond that they have broken up a dangerous criminal organization. Reports have accused the chief of police of going after certain criminal organizations in order to favor others, however.

Tijuana, with a population of five million, is part of a transnational metropolis that includes Rosarito, Tecate and San Diego (U.S.A.). It displays a major asymmetry with regard to the U.S. border, having expanded over a valley and a mesa and through hills, canyons, ravines, riverbeds and canals. Its prevailing sign is the struggle for territory. Adriana Ruiz crossed paths with organized crime, which, thanks to its illicit enterprises, is in at least partial possession of the city's territory. The media and the transmedia find their influence as a means of flattening an uneven territory, triggering an immediate, simultaneous, ubiquitous reaction among institutional actors. The formality of the institutions is pushed aside by the alegal haste unleashed by public opinion. The victim is murdered more than once: first in real life, then as a sensationalistic news story and finally with the potential dissemination of the recording made by the criminals. The victim enters a cycle of continuous revictimization. Her path takes her from the center of Tijuana society to its margins, a path that comes to its end in a garbage dump on the outskirts of the city.

Body/person of Genaro Macías:[7] a used car salesman from Zamora, Michoacán and the father of two. His economic situation has improved in recent years. He works with two of his brothers: Ulises and Pedro. He is kidnapped one day while driving around town. They take him to a safe house, address unknown. His family negotiates the ransom payment. One month after the kidnapping, the victim is released. He stays with relatives, who urge him to leave the country. He would be safe in the United States. The victim refuses. After several weeks in hiding, he gets himself ready and says farewell to his children, his wife and the rest of his family. There are men waiting for him outside. He's kidnapped again. His body is found soon afterwards on the outskirts of the city, near the highway to Guadalajara. Beside it lie the bodies of his two brothers. The victims are naked from the waist up and their bodies show signs of torture. Genaro Macías has been given the *coup de grace* and the letter 'Z' has been carved into his forehead. The police inform the press that these murders have been committed by the Zetas, who executed the victims for having betrayed their criminal organization, dealing with their rivals for control of the region: La Familia.

Zamora is located in a valley and is a pole of economic activity based around fruit cultivation and exportation—primarily blackberries and strawberries—as well as the service sector that meets the needs of its population of 300,000. Its place name, of Iberian origin, means "walled city." Zamora is currently a zone of open transit between the state capitals of Guadalajara (Jalisco) and Morelia (Michoacán). Zamora's sign is territorial fluidity, interrupted only by traffic blockades in urban areas, a tactic used by criminal organizations to pressure the authorities. The victim and his brothers fell into the convergence of business with organized crime: the sale of used cars is a common means of laundering money. By involving himself in illicit cash flows, the victim's path became one of extreme risk.

Body/person of Daniel Arteaga:[8] born in Martínez de la Torre, Veracruz but a resident of Mexico State and the father of a daughter studying abroad in Europe. He analyzes and executes civil intelligence operations for the Mexican government. His experience and honesty are acknowledged by his peers, both civilian and military, as well as by intelligence agencies in the United States, Europe and Israel. The dismantlement of Mexico's intelligence agencies during the first decade of the 21st century and their reconfiguration around the Public Security Secretariat (SSP) in the fight against drug trafficking from 2007 on has meant that, despite his proven honesty and experience, his responsibilities have been reduced. In the course of his duties, he uncovers many cases of corruption, negligence and criminal oversight on the part of police officers and government functionaries at the highest levels of the SSP. He decides to report this by addressing a letter to the president. The response is silence. One day, his doorbell rings: he finds a suitcase. He opens it; it's full of money. He takes the suitcase and goes to the office of the person he believes sent it: his superior in the chain of command. He hands over the suitcase, but is given a choice: either take the money or resign, or else he will be killed along with his entire family. He resigns. He will work as a private intelligence consultant for state governments.

The corruption of Mexico's security and intelligence sectors impedes progress. There is no corner of the country where this problem does not exist. Thanks to his character and experience, a government functionary like Daniel Arteaga represents an obstacle to the alegal development of the new public security architecture: he has gone from the heart of intelligence activities to the institutional margins to the extent that anomalies have multiplied within the country's control, surveillance and policing apparatus. This institutional degradation has been ubiquitous and simultaneous and is far from being a focused, correctible problem: the SSP is a dysfunctional agency. On the margins, his days are numbered.

Body/person of Elías Castillo:[9] a political correspondent who invests his money in side businesses and resides in the city of Veracruz, on the Gulf of Mexico. A well-known individual in political circles in Veracruz, one day he is kidnapped on the street. They take him to an unknown safe house where a man in a ski mask talks with him for days on end while his family and friends negotiate the ransom payment. Thanks to their surveillance of the victim and their interception of his mail and electronic communications, the kidnappers know his routine inside and out. Apart from the ransom, they also ask him to give them his house. The victim responds that he's still paying off his mortgage: by handing over the deed, he'd only be passing on a debt. The news of the kidnapping reaches the press. The victim's family and friends begin to collect the ransom money. The kidnappers release him. A man in a ski mask tells him that they're only letting him go because they have the same friends in political circles. The victim knows that he may be kidnapped again at any time and starts thinking about leaving the city.

Criminal spaces have become indistinguishable from political spaces. As organized crime has vast knowledge of their assets and their field of activity, potential victims are subjected to a systematic plan of pursuit and attack that expands in a centrifugal pattern. With no distinction between the legal and the illegal, the paths of those operating in the world of crime and in the world of politics intertwine. The victim witnesses a contraction of their living space that corresponds to the expansion of criminal space. Wherever organized crime dominates, the division between public life and private life disappears. The victim becomes a prisoner. Or a parolee.

Body/person of Jesús Torrijos:[10] a group of soldiers enter his house in Ciudad Juárez, Chihuahua after midnight with neither a search warrant nor a warrant for his arrest. They loot his house, stealing money and taking him prisoner. His wife reports the incident to the Human Rights Commission of the State of Chihuahua and provides cellphone videos of the damage caused by the soldiers. The army states that the arrest was made three days before it actually occurred: in their report, they state that they had approached Torrijos on the street and arrested him on the spot when they saw him throw away a baggie of marijuana. Torrijos is charged with crimes against public health and possession with intent to sell. During his trial, the incoherence of the army's account becomes clear. The victim is released three months later, but the judge fails to order an investigation into the soldiers' alleged crimes: abuse of authority, theft, assault, torture. Nor does the prosecutor show any interest in these crimes.

The violation of the human rights and constitutional rights of victims by soldiers opens up another dimension of the state's alegal convergence with organized crime. For victims, caught between the extreme violence of the armed forces and that of organized crime, the constituted order disappears. The exhaustion of legality divides the legal status of persons. Legal omissions by the authorities themselves hinder the enforcement of the law and the pursuit of justice. The rule of law becomes the rule of crime.

Body/person of Eliud Naranjo:[11] a 33-year-old municipal police officer, he is arrested at 8:45 a.m. by a score of soldiers and police officers who barge into his home in Huimanguillo, Tabasco. The security forces beat him in front of his family. They blindfold him and take him away in an unidentified vehicle to an unknown place. They torture him until he agrees to confess to working for a criminal organization. Police reports state that Naranjo was arrested *in flagrante delicto* at a checkpoint near Cárdenas, Tabasco. In their "narrative account of the incident," the arresting officers declare that they saw him following a police convoy in a "suspicious" manner and that Naranjo "spontaneously" confessed to working for a criminal organization. Naranjo denies the charges against him: he alleges that he was arbitrarily arrested and tortured into giving a false confession. Nevertheless, he remains in prison while awaiting appeal.

The authorities produce a "narrative" that rewrites the facts to cover up violations of the human rights of the victims. The construction of this narrative is a repeated *modus operandi* and the authorities work closely with police officers and prosecutors in a premeditated, concerted fashion when bringing charges against someone. Far from following the principle of due process, the judge adheres to a procedural rigidity that doesn't take substantive issues of impartiality, justice and freedom into consideration. The edifice of the law becomes a tortuous place for victims from the moment they enter it.

Body/person of José Barrera:[12] the owner of a glass shop on the outskirts of Ciudad Juárez, though he is originally from Durango. He founded his business in 1995 and has managed to become a homeowner with a higher standard of living than his neighbors. He surrounds himself with relatives from his hometown who have moved to the border city in search of work. Gangsters enter his shop one morning. They try to extort him, but the victim, as he has done during previous extortion attempts, refuses to hand over any money. They shoot him, as they have done at the neighborhood's corner store and stationary shop. When she hears the gunshots, his wife runs to the shop, which is located next to their two-story home. By the time she reaches him, he's already dead. The police take the victim's body away and more than a day goes by before they release it to the family: murders tend to be seen as the result of the victim's ties to organized crime. His wife and six children, all of them minors, along with the rest of his family, are forced to close the glass shop and leave Ciudad Juárez.

The neighborhoods of Ciudad Juárez are dominated by gangs who extort residents: the police accept this and protect their regime, which functions as an illegal government. The exploitation of movement and space and the profit from illegal enterprises determine the rules of coexistence in the border city's neighborhoods. Citizens are included in the apparently normal functioning of society, which is in fact a vast prison, as the streets and avenues are only relatively peaceful during the day. Normally only police officers and gangsters are out on the street at night. For regular citizens, the risk of going out at night is too high. Private spaces have ceased to exist as such: gangsters can make their appearance at any moment; there are no walls, barriers or limits that can contain them and private space has become yet another field of operations for their illegal enterprises. The illegal devours the legal and the formal economy is absorbed by the informal, underground economy. Under the domination of organized crime and the government's struggle against it, urban territory transforms into a daily warzone comparable to other low-intensity conflicts.

Body/person of Rodolfo Nájera:[13] a police officer from Lerdo, Coahuila. He appears in a video, facing the camera. Two masked men with assault rifles stand guard. The victim is kneeling, his hands tied behind his back, his face badly beaten and his left eye swollen. His left ear has been ripped half off. He's being questioned by a voice from offscreen. The victim confesses that he works for two drug traffickers known as El Pirata and El Delta. His interrogator forces him to reveal the network of criminals and police officers to which he belongs. The victim recounts a series of events that occurred in the city of Torreón, Coahuila, near the northern border with Texas. Some time before, a group of armed men had attacked three bars in Torreón, killing 10 people and wounding 40. Later on, a different Torreón bar was assaulted, leaving eight people dead and another 20 wounded. Weeks later, a private party at a Torreón hotel was crashed by five men with bulletproof vests and assault rifles, who fired on the partygoers; 17 people were killed and another 18 were wounded. After each massacre, the killers recrossed the state line between

Coahuila and Durango and returned to their prison cells in Gómez Palacio. These criminals operated with the approval and protection of the warden. In the video, the victim appears in another location. Another brief dialogue takes place. The offscreen voice asks the victim if his men prefer to kill innocents because they're unable to confront the last letter: the Zetas. The victim responds: Yes, sir. The voice insists: You can't defeat us. The victim agrees: We can't. The men guarding him walk offscreen. A shot rings out. The victim falls forward. The video is disseminated on social media the next day. The authorities arrest the prison warden and the sicarios.

The police are sold to the highest bidder. Criminal organizations are a superinstitutional power that finds it just as easy to break out of prison as it is to move from one place to another. Investigations into crimes tend to be subsumed into the world of organized crime, which violates institutional limitations and imposes its own law of revenge or retributive justice: *lex talionis*. Cruelty and a lack of respect for human rights are the norm for organized crime and legality is overwhelmed by illegality. The use of video increases the panic of the victims and the arrogance of the victimizers: transmediatic spaces multiply the possibilities for aggression by criminal organizations, which bring together the real, the mediatic and the transmediatic under one abject precept. A perverse, deformed vision is imposed on spectators and the general public, a report on the defenselessness of the victim: anamorphosis, the unsayable. An involution of cultural space.

Body/person of José Antonio Elena:[14] a 16-year-old resident of Nogales, Sonora, which borders Nogales, Arizona. He is shot down along the border. The U.S. Border Patrol states that the minor and three other suspects were transporting marijuana into U.S. territory. When they were caught, they ran to take refuge in Mexico. From behind the border wall, a Border Patrol agent shot at the victim eight times: two bullets were found in his head and four in his throat; the other bullets were lodged in the wall of a doctor's office near where his body lay. The minor had been throwing rocks at the Border Patrol agents to distract them and was then killed by one of these same agents. A Border Patrol spokesman states that when a person, an agent, feels that their life is in danger, or that of another agent or other person—read here U.S. citizen—the border does not exist.

The border is subject to the logic of war. In wartime and on the field of battle, a soldier or agent of the United States has the obligation to defend their country and their way of life, in accordance with the Code of the United States Fighting

Force.[15] The U.S. government considers drug trafficking to be a crime comparable to terrorism and terrorists lack rights, as they are considered to be "enemy combatants" and are therefore outside the scope of the Geneva Convention.[16] The mere suspicion of a threat to the national security of the United States on the part of the country's soldiers and agents is enough to justify action and the consequences of this action will be defended by the U.S. government. A maxim imposes itself: *Inter arma silent leges*, in times of war, the law falls silent.[17] Submission, destruction, extermination.

The field of battle approaches the problem of reality in all its forces, tensions, pressures, events, conditions, factors and opportunities. From the perspective of ultracontemporary military thinking, there are two concepts that are of use here: friction, describing that which, despite the best-laid plans, creates resistance on the ground; and fog, which refers to the ambiguity and uncertain knowledge of actors in a combat situation. Military actors often speak of the "fog and friction" of war.[18] The anamorphosis of the victims arises from the frictive, foggy experience of the threshold between war and peace. In the field of battle, nature and even space itself are victimized.[19]

To explain the meaning of anamorphosis, let us imagine the victim faced with a situation that can be divided into two phases: first there is their habitual reality, which is then violated by a traumatic event that, in the cases we have described, involves the intervention of a criminal agent or an act of war; afterwards, the victim begins to perceive events and their own person from a deformed perspective: they are no longer the person they were before the criminal or military intervention, even when their memory insists to the contrary. The entire criminal or military episode in which the victim is enmeshed represents an anamorphosis. The object of their desire is the restoration of normality. The oblique gaze that allows the common observer to enjoy an anamorphosis in a painting[20] is impossible: they would have to be situated outside the scene. The victim has become an anamorphosis incarnate. Their desire to restore their habitual time and space expresses the opposite: shock, the edge of the void, the nothingness that slowly emerges from the extreme deformation they experience before dying (even if this death is suspended or dilated by contingency or inertia).

If we compare the experience of the victim with the classic example of anamorphosis, Hans Holbein the Younger's painting *The Ambassadors* (1533),[21] the victim would be situated within the distorted skull at the feet of the subjects, which represents the supremacy of death over worldly vanity. In the case of filmed murders and atrocities, the anamorphosis of the victim emerges as a possible variation on scopophilia: the compulsive, pleasurable contemplation of something perceived as sinister. The victim of an anomalous event dematerializes, becoming nothing more than a fantasy, a morbid fascination or an obsession for the observer. Everyday normality is reconstituted through the pleasure, self-absorption or panic of the other, the concealed observer who is always outside the frame.

For the victimizer, this anamorphosis is invisible, as the acts of cruelty and transgression they commit constitute their objective world: an incarnation of evil. From their perspective, the victim lacks all value and is nothing more than an object for whatever depravations arise from their desire for supremacy. The theatricality of their abuses and sacrifices ignore any considerations beyond capturing, preying upon or annihilating their victim. An anamorphic figure unable to view themselves as such. The only human trait left to the victimizer is their anonymity. A nameless face, masked or hooded, that takes refuge in deformity; they yearn for erasure, negation. The acute terror of being discovered and punished.

If the victim is engulfed in the anamorphosis constructed by the violence exercised upon them, then the victimizer seeks to become invisible as a person and to remain alive by exterminating others. Both are united by the confluence that led their paths or destinies to tragically intertwine.

Criminal groups dedicated to drug trafficking and other illicit enterprises have two strategic advantages over the armed forces that combat them and, therefore, over their potential victims: 1) a direct understanding of the territories they occupy, which they obtain from both knowledge and experience: they plan and undertake actions and, at the same time, flatten or aim to flatten the area in which they are undertaken; and 2) the development of combat networks using telecommunications and clientelistic or community employment relationships that improve the efficacy of their logistical and tactical operations. Organized crime implies a variant of Fourth Generation Warfare (4GW), which makes use of political, economic, social and military networks in order to convince the enemy that their strategic objectives are either unattainable or only obtainable at too great a cost.[22]

The consequence of all this is a reformulation of ideas of space and territory, which become protean and take on new forms as criminal organizations pass through, dominate or control them, such as with the checkpoints at the entrance to a town. Criminal groups function as highly flexible, organized units: they either reject established, linear routes altogether or rotate them with ever-changing alternatives through mountain passes or other unusual routes that often make use of swarming tactics: a diffuse multiplicity of small units, coordinated but virtually autonomous, acting with comprehensive synergy.[23] The direct result of these types of operations is a spatial malleability that affects the territory and localities under their influence to the point at which the conventional map is altered to suit their ends, goals and objectives, for example, when tactical blockades involving human, communication, clientelistic and employment networks are set up to isolate and protect criminal groups from possible attacks by the armed forces.[24]

The field of battle is a medium transformed by its operations: a flexible, almost liquid material that remains dependent on events, its conventional state one of suspense.[25] An oscillation between rest and perpetual motion that imposes an ever-expanding instability.

This imposition also modifies community customs and traditions. People, as potential victims, have three options: affiliating themselves with the criminal group, either temporarily or permanently; marginalization; exile. The drug war produces hundreds of thousands of exiles fleeing from criminal domains. And if everyday space is deformed by criminal groups, the same occurs with the organization and administration of time: not only do gangs and other criminal organizations break down walls, borders, limits, entrances and exits, they also act in a fragmented, simultaneous fashion in multiple directions, confusing any linear chronology; they are unpredictable, dispersed and unstable, finding favor in asymmetry, synchronization and chaos.[26]

Criminal groups utilize the element of surprise, which increases the terror felt by their potential victims: rumor, scandal, the noise made about one's self form a communicative loop that becomes parasitic as it repeats itself.[27] The anticipation of terror as a psychological element becomes another weapon in their arsenal that is made even more powerful by the ineffectiveness of the armed forces. The immediate effect, above all if the armed forces lack respect for human rights, is a rejection by the population of legality and the constituted powers, making them indirect accomplices of organized crime.

The flattening of space and territory have become highly sophisticated: criminal groups suddenly appear, imposing a new flatness on the terrain, even on rugged mountain ranges, as they connect strategic points through their own means of communication,[28] disregarding the line between legality and illegality and collapsing the real and symbolic divisions between the public and the private. A series of commando units, for example, will block traffic in an urban area: they simultaneously or successively occupy intersections or the roads leading into town, robbing vehicles and setting them on fire, thus attracting and engaging the armed forces. They then flee, leaving behind ruins, victims and terror. They paralyze metropolitan areas with thousands and even millions of inhabitants, such as Guadalajara, Monterrey, Nuevo Laredo, Torreón, Matamoros, Veracruz, Reynosa, etc. Communities suddenly find themselves immersed in an emergent homogeneity and planimetry.

A war zone is a mandate for absolute dispossession. In the alienation of experience, victims face the threat of the anomalous or traumatic situation or episode. As the homogeneity or planimetry imposed by criminals or the armed forces normalizes itself, there is a curtailment of reality and its elemental signs. And the humanity of a person is objectified and reduced to their usefulness or uselessness for criminal activities, or to collateral damage on the part of the armed forces. The life world for those subjected to criminal domination or to the fight against crime tends to be emptied out and replaced with impositions, rules and the whims of criminals. Without this emptiness, there would be no anamorphosis of the victims, who glimpse a threat from their first contact—whether direct or indirect—with organized crime or government authority. And this feeds their deepest fears—a secret passageway symbolically opens up between reality and subjectivity.

Emergent Space

Legal omissions by the authorities themselves hinder the enforcement of the law and the pursuit of justice. The rule of law becomes the rule of crime.

A war zone is a mandate for absolute dispossession. In the alienation of experience, victims face the threat of the anomalous or traumatic situation or episode.

Communities suddenly find themselves immersed in an emergent homogeneity and planimetry.

The flattening of space and territory have become highly sophisticated: criminal groups suddenly appear, imposing a new flatness on the terrain, even on rugged mountain ranges, as they connect strategic points through their own means of communication, disregarding the line between legality and illegality and collapsing the real and symbolic divisions between the public and the private.

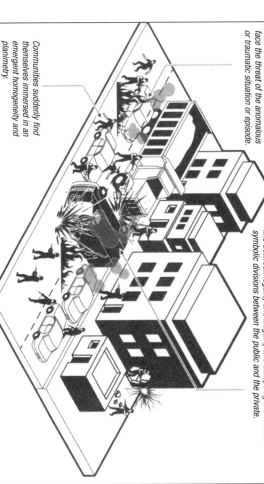

Faced with the threat of violence and an uncontested power that breaks down all barriers, people undergo an extreme transformation: notions of time and space are subjected to an inverted or perverse regime that gives rise to an abject architecture altering known values and imposing a reality of contiguous spaces controlled and watched over by organized crime or the armed forces. People become prone to agoraphobia (danger as external) or claustrophobia (danger as internal). Citizens become unsure of themselves, living in a prolonged state of uncertainty: the climate of friction and fog.

A person remains invisible as long as the field of battle allows it; once they become visible and objective, they enter a state of anamorphosis, which also contains an aspect of transgression. In the face of this transgression, the person looks and feels increasingly defenseless. The transgression or rupture of the conventional order produces monsters and monstrosities.[29]

As part of their flattening or leveling of space and time, criminals employ a peculiar form of transgression, one endowed with its own symbolisms, contents, myths, images, icons and representations, which are derived from both vernacular culture and the culture of the mass media: music, radio, film. And from messages circulated on social media: exaltations of crime, thuggish arrogance, testimonies of cruelty, affirmations of illegality, celebrations of criminal exploits, recollections of the criminal life, etc. Transgressive fantasies that constitute a liturgy against the constituted order invade real space with their practical consequences, furthering the imperative towards homogeneity and flatness—the reality, in other words, of crime in the absence of limits—and incorporating the imaginary of the monstrous: the cruel carnival that inverts the conventional world.

There then proliferate displays of military strength, representations of groups or regions, peculiar appearances, signs distinguishing one from one's rivals, forms and fashions that differentiate them from both common people and the armed forces that pursue them, which in turn have their own tastes in imagery and their own propaganda or communicative flatness.[30]

Both real and symbolic space are invaded by this criminal transgression, which produces not only symbolism (emblems, uniforms, masks, tattoos, etc.) but also tools, artifacts, vehicles, buildings that bear the identifying marks of different criminal organizations. Their use value also contains the added value provided by the forms that give meaning or meaninglessness to their transgressive actions.

Each object produced by criminals bears the mark of its provenance, as criminal objects combine utility and ornamentation in equal proportions. And they mirror their origins: transgressive, monstrous, tangible omens, their very existence is intimidating. Their immobility is threatening; their movement, lethal. In them, individuals see a premonition of anamorphosis.

One example of this is the design of the all-terrain vehicles used by criminal groups, especially those that have been transformed from civilian to combat use. Armored plating is manufactured at specialized garages, along with other additions and adaptations made at a low cost (ten to fifteen thousand dollars).[31] From being vehicles for cargo or general transportation, these trucks become assault tanks and armored transports, protecting criminal assets and troops. This armoring, which consists of added iron parts and steel plating with a high degree of resistance (capable of withstanding a bazooka blast), is complemented by bulletproof tires and reinforced glass windows, as well as spotlights for nighttime operations and turrets or openings for artillery and other weapons. These vehicles take on monstrous forms that parody industrial war material (tanks, armored cars, amphibious assault vehicles) and accept their artisanal-vernacular origins in the fantasies of criminal groups and their symbolisms of power, intimidation, efficacy, invulnerability and defiance of the rules of coexistence.

Faced with the mere presence of such vehicles, potential victims must imagine that even the armed forces could find themselves at a disadvantage. Created for clashes with rival criminal organizations as well, these vehicles can even be equipped with devices that discharge electric shocks or help them avoid pursuers (by scattering sharp metal objects behind them or releasing pepper spray or tear gas). According to the authorities, the weakness of these vehicles is their slowness (40 to 50 kilometers per hour), their heaviness, their tires and their appearance, as they are readily identifiable from a distance by either land-based or aerial surveillance.

In rural areas, they have the advantage on level roads and paths; they are difficult to drive in urban areas and so their presence is much more in terms of their symbolic meaning than their real use. They are tools of intimidation and psychological impact that communicate a perception of absolute power through their sculptural appearance, which references the massive force and energy of the industrial era and the machinery, imaginary and culture of heavy metal music, horror films and postapocalyptic fiction.[32] The reduction of reality to the message of the supremacy of the strong puts the victim in anamorphic perspective. The impression of a mobile power that breaks down all barriers creates panic in the community and, perhaps, among rival groups. If we examine the form of these vehicles, which are built by a variety of criminal groups, we can find certain similarities: an alternation between symmetry and asymmetry, points (with all their phallic associations), trapezoids, the front section as a terrible mask, turrets and their aspirations of being a mobile fortress, a dark or rusty surface, a rough finish. Taken together, these forms imply the embodiment of criminal fantasies and an imperative to reduce combat potential in favor of an apotropaic effect: the replacement of the real with faith in a symbolic defense based around superstition or premodern thinking, in which certain actions, gestures, rituals, objects or liturgical phrases have the power to prevent, dispel or deflect evil or some material or immaterial threat, or to create a protective shield against demons, evil spirits or black magic. These armored vehicles are gigantic, mobile amulets that, apart from their utility, seek to process the fears they provoke and concentrate around them. Aggressive toys that find their deepest purpose, in terms of criminal operations and the territorial and spatial domination of organized crime, in their indirect effect on potential victims. The armed forces of the constituted order, in turn, operate under the logic of the strong state, of terror and war. On the threshold of horror, we encounter the bodies of persons and their vulnerable perimeters.

4

GLOBAL WAR ON DRUG TRAFFICKING

Over the course of the first decade of the 21st century, Mexican drug cartels have only gotten more powerful. The international prestige of Mexican drug traffickers is a sign of the failure of the government's war on organized crime. The government makes arrests and seizes contraband while violence and insecurity increase and illicit business booms. In 2003, Mexican drug traffickers became the leaders in transporting drugs from South America to the United States, which continues to be the world's largest drug consumption market.[1] Supremacy in Mexico opens up access to other continents, hence the bitterness of the conflict.

The decisive factor that allowed for their rise has been the ineffectiveness and corruption of the government institutions involved in the struggle against drug trafficking. This struggle has become an unsolvable problem for Mexico's government and is starting to become a challenge for Europe and the rest of the Americas as well. According to

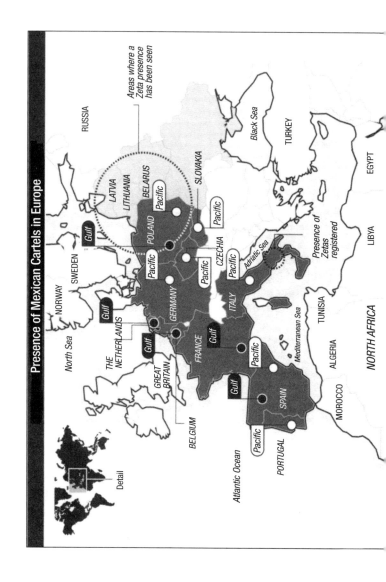

Presence of Mexican Cartels in Europe

Areas where a Zeta presence has been seen

Presence of Zetas registered

RUSSIA

LATVIA

LITHUANIA

BELARUS

Pacific

SLOVAKIA

Pacific

POLAND

Pacific

Gulf

CZECHIA

Pacific

Black Sea

TURKEY

SWEDEN

NORWAY

North Sea

GERMANY

Pacific

ITALY

Adriatic Sea

EGYPT

THE NETHERLANDS

Gulf

Gulf

GREAT BRITAIN

BELGIUM

FRANCE

Gulf

Pacific

Mediterranean Sea

TUNISIA

LIBYA

NORTH AFRICA

Atlantic Ocean

Pacific

PORTUGAL

SPAIN

Gulf

MOROCCO

ALGERIA

Detail

the United Nations Office on Drugs and Crime (UNODC), the cocaine produced in Colombia, Peru and Bolivia for consumption in Europe is transported by Mexican drug traffickers, who have slowly displaced the Colombians and compete with the Venezuelans over trafficking routes to Europe, particularly those that utilize West Africa. It's estimated that 90% of the drugs that reach the European continent are transported via this route.

Mexican drug cartels have a presence in 38 countries in Europe, Africa and the Middle East and their expansion has been a cause for alarm for the authorities in Spain, Germany and Italy, making clear the failure of the governments of the Americas.[2]

Mexican drug traffickers have made a name for themselves in intercontinental transport and have already supplanted the Colombians as the world's biggest distributors of narcotics. In 2008, over 200 people were arrested in the United States and Italy after a connection was uncovered between the Zetas and the Italian 'Ndrangheta, whose criminal enterprises have an annual revenue of 55 billion dollars. The Mexicans, who are very effective and very violent, bring cocaine from Colombia to New York, and from there it's taken to Italy.[3]

The United Nations has warned that drug trafficking is more than the mere transportation of drugs: it implies other criminal industries (money laundering, kidnapping, extortion, theft, human trafficking, gun running, etc.). And generalized violence. The case of Latin America is alarming because it reveals the future that threatens Europe. As a whole, Latin America and the Caribbean have the highest rates of violence in the world.[4] This is due to the fact that drug trafficking requires a large arsenal and its violence extends beyond those who participate in drug trafficking activities. A lethal infection for the established order.

The central problem is that, through corruption, Mexico's public and private institutions have strengthened the rise of gangs and drug cartels. This crisis in the rule of law reveals the dark side of the global order: the underground economy, whose politics consist of violence.[5] Blood, death, intimidation, exploitation, ammunition, endless profit. The enormity of the drug business has led experts to increasingly question their continued illegality, instead proposing an end to the global policy of prohibition as a possible solution to this problem.[6]

Mexico lives between the memory of its past revolutions and the reality of its current state of regression: the retreat of the rule of law in the face of the biggest crisis in its contemporary history.

In the state of Tamaulipas, on the Gulf of Mexico, the bodies of 72 Central American migrants were found on a ranch near the U.S.

border. According to the official report, they were executed by the Zetas. Murders of migrants are common along that route. In Colima, on the Pacific coast, a former governor was assassinated, as was a gubernatorial candidate in Tamaulipas. And the massacres, decapitations and dismemberments between criminal groups never let up.[7]

The achievements of the authorities in the fight against drug trafficking can be seen in the many military operations that have left bystanders dead. In 2010, there was also an operation in Tamaulipas that left roughly one hundred people dead, both criminals and civilians, among them a local reporter; at the beginning of the 21st century, Mexico became one of the most dangerous countries in the world for journalists.[8]

The National Human Rights Commission has reported a nearly 500% increase in the number of reports of human rights abuses committed by soldiers and police officers since the start of the war against drug trafficking in 2006. To justify its policies, the Mexican government has said, "If you see dust in the air, it's because we're cleaning house."

The crisis of insecurity and violence in Mexico reveals the irresponsibility and incompetence of the government and the ruling class, as well as their rupture with society itself in their strategy of confrontation in defense of the established order. As is well known, the country's institutional erosion began two decades before and has been on the rise ever since 2000.

The basis of the Mexican strategy was to incorporate the army into police work across the country, followed by the navy, in an operational vanguard. The objective has been to militarize society. The result has been a rise in violence across the country. Mexico has never been as unsafe as it is now, as it deploys its human and material resources like never before in its history to fight criminal violence.

According to the Mexican Senate, organized crime dominates 71% of the country's territory.[9] And this power is not only far from retreating, but has even diversified, expanding into other criminal industries: kidnapping, extortion, robbery, human trafficking, cargo theft and street-level drug sales across Mexico.

The arrests of drug lords and sicarios, which the authorities have turned into a propagandistic spectacle, have done little to affect the operations of drug cartels, as they're immediately replaced. Or new groups arise: the balkanization of Mexico is already underway.[10]

The struggle against organized crime has been on Mexico's political agenda for 25 years now. Ineffectiveness and corruption have marked a strategy destined to fail. Besides erring in its diagnosis of the situation and in its method of combat, the Mexican government has started from five false premises: 1) considering organized crime to be an agent external to the country's institutions instead of something inherent to them; 2) reducing the problem to a matter for criminologists and the police, in which the complexity of drug trafficking and its associated criminal industries are on one side and the state's security forces on the other (on the contrary, they have often coexisted and maintained a certain dialogue, pressuring some groups to fight others for control of markets, territories and transportation routes); 3) covering up the degradation of the country's police forces, government institutions, courts and prisons, as well as its most serious consequence: Mexico's absolute impunity rate (93–99% of crimes go unpunished);[11] 4) avoiding the status of drug trafficking as a geopolitical problem for the United States, in which its government tends to apply a double standard in accordance with its national security interests; 5) ignoring that a war's theater of operations is always broader than the localities in which violence occurs, such as Ciudad Juárez.

As the crisis reaches ever higher degrees of violence, the government and the ruling class refuse to change their way of thinking. The lie that this violence is proof of the effectiveness of the government's offensive falls apart under its own weight. What's worse is that public and private life have been militarized as the result of an erroneous strategy: the war machine as yet one more omen of future regression.

Drug trafficking has corrupted the institutions responsible for enforcing the law and ensuring justice, as well as federal intelligence agencies, the armed forces, the police, state governments, political parties, the judicial system, the capital and the banking and financial systems. Never have so many suffered for so few.[12]

In Latin America, organized crime has become entangled with the institutions of every country due to the corrupting influence of drug cartels—above all those from Mexico—and gangs, which are increasingly influential across the region and which have very important ties to the economies of the United States and the European Union.[13] The UN has warned of the growing demand for drugs in Africa and Latin America, where governments lack the capacity to deal with the social consequences of drug addiction. Rich countries have imposed drug consumption on poor countries alongside their production and trafficking. This transference is doubly perverse, as it sows social instability and the risk of criminal insurgency.

The solutions that tend to be proposed are the same in every country and always follow the doctrine of drug prohibition. An incriminating, repressive policy based on the use of violence by the government. The project of militarizing society begins with the establishment of a single national police force, concentrating and centralizing command under the Interior Ministry, which in turn answers to more powerful governments or international agencies. This threatens local autonomy and deepens another project of military integration: that of Mexico with the United States. These measures, proposed as a "solution," only complicate a matter of serious global impact.

The formal conduct of the United States towards Mexico and the drug problem has evolved over the decades: a historic phase of tolerance (1920–1969), prohibitionist tolerance (1969–1985), punitive prohibition (1985–1989) and binational cooperation and U.S. certification of Mexico's war on drug trafficking (1989–2002). Between 2002 and 2006, drug trafficking became an urgent issue for both countries, leading to a war on drug trafficking in Mexico based around U.S. national security principles.[14]

The meanings of space, region and territory have been evolving ever since the rise of the global economy and the emergence of information societies. Borders, as regions of strategic tension, have become porous, malleable, conductive and fluid, to a large degree due to the phenomenon of human migration.[15] The war machine and the criminal machine feed off of borders due to two factors: human trafficking and arms trafficking.

Since September 11th, 2001, the United States has considered its southern border with Mexico to be a national security priority, which has exacerbated the traditional tensions between the two countries. Despite plans to erect a wall along the entire border, the U.S. government admitted in 2011 that it only had effective control over 15% of the border, with only an operational response capacity over the rest.[16] Its "fortifications" proved to be precarious. In 2013, on the pretext of an immigration reform, the U.S. Senate voted to strengthen border security by doubling the number of police officers, extending fences and acquiring additional surveillance equipment, such as cameras, vehicles, helicopters and drones.

Against the old conception of borders as static national boundaries, today they are flexible and liquid. This results in the reciprocal penetration of both cultures. The new fabric of the border produces a transborder, creating translinear spaces that alter meanings and representations of function and identity, as well as giving rise to emergent temporalities, configurations and mutations.[17] Each side of the border interacts with the other and transforms itself in the process: they clash, dialogue, repel and fuse, either temporarily or permanently.

Along the border between Mexico and the United States, this could be seen since the 1960s, when the maquiladora industry took off and migratory flows began to focus on the region. Four decades later, the results of this global-local anomaly are clear: a territory that, on the Mexican side (Ciudad Juárez, for example), has experienced unequal, mixed, unstable and unrestrained development, deeply affecting its economy, politics, society and culture. And it shares a border with El Paso, the second-safest city in the United States.[18] These contrasts also feed xenophobia north of the Río Grande. Along the border, there are more than 12,000 points of sale for weapons that are banned in Mexico.[19] This has led many to believe that the basic dynamic of the Mexican crisis is a strategic maneuver on the part of the United States: drugs for guns. This business has variants: on the pretext of tracing their illegal circulation, the Bureau of Alcohol, Tobacco, Firearms and Explosives (ATF) permitted thousands of arms to be sold to criminals in Mexico between 2009 and 2010.[20]

The border through this shared desert faces the threat of pure barbarism, or at the very least, institutional anomalies. The signs are in the folds and creases of the border region: in the culture that endures and in the microphysics of everyday life. Its translinear spaces can be interpreted through three images that are recurrent along the border, both concretely and symbolically: the bridge, the wall and the garbage dump. The international bridge functions as a safety valve controlling the flow of people looking for work in the United States, as well as the traffic in drugs and weapons; the wall, more implied than concrete, is a failed defensive barrier against the liquidity and porosity of the transborder; the garbage dump represents the most highly developed product of that sinister ecology that converts the cities of a developing country into the garbage dump or backyard of the developed country on the other side of the border. History proves this.

Mexico's degradation began in the heart of its institutions. The criminal machine of drug trafficking in Mexico is consubstantial with the country's political and economic institutions. And the United States is implicated as well. Mexico's adverse situation at the beginning of the 21st century has been gestating for years, dating back to the pacts the government made with various criminal organizations.[21] These pacts constitute the origin of today's cartels, compromising the country's territory in the South American drug trade in exchange for money. This ended up corrupting the police, the armed forces, the economy, politics and society.

These agreements were an extension of Mexico's support for the U.S.-led operations carried out in its territory as part of the Iran/Contra affair, which began in 1981. These operations, which consisted of supplying Nicaraguan counterrevolutionaries with weapons in exchange for drugs for the U.S. market, were conceived and executed by the CIA, which even planned and carried out assassinations of those who knew about these operations at the time and threatened to reveal them. Operations in Mexican territory were the responsibility of the agency's domestic counterpart: the Federal Security Directorate.

In recent decades, the U.S. has sponsored or induced democratic change in Latin America. In terms of social progress, the results have been few and far between, and instead there has been a proliferation of poverty, marginalization and organized crime, particularly drug trafficking in all its anti-institutional power.

For the U.S., control over Mexico and Central America occurs in the context of the crises of the region's countries, allowing for the paramilitarization of their territories—including mercenaries on Pentagon payroll—as well as that of a booming arms industry and the intelligence or punitive operations conducted on behalf of American interests. Once again, free trade and regional security agreements have been arranged.[22] The historical precedents from around the world are very telling on this point.[23] Drug trafficking and related criminal industries serve as a pretext for the comprehensive geopolitical strategy of the United States, which consists of the application of two military concepts to the civilian world: command and control, achieved through doctrine, organization, training and education.[24] Technology is at the center of all this. In their first phase, these notions have two points of diffusion and subcontinental impact: Mexico (Central America) and Colombia (South America). And, among others, there is one fundamental objective: fighting terrorism.

The U.S. government has upheld the hypothesis of a possible alliance between Al Qaeda and certain Mexican drug cartels. Mexico has denied this.[25] In 2011, the U.S. insisted on a potential alliance between Al Qaeda and the Zetas, a group of sicarios who grew to the point where they were able to establish their own intercontinental criminal enterprise.[26]

The Zetas were founded by deserters from the Mexican Army who had received elite training in Mexico and the U.S. The Western Hemisphere Institute for Security Cooperation, formerly known as the School of the Americas, has been the traditional site at which the Pentagon and U.S. intelligence agencies recruit Latin American military officials for secret operations whose objective is to impose a strategy of domination without direct military occupation. Or rather, to combat threats like terrorism and radical populism.

Through intelligence analyses based on its geopolitical prospects, the U.S. remains alert to developments south of the border. And it has warned of the unprecedented level of violence exercised by Mexican cartels in their crimes and turf wars. It will defend this war on drug trafficking until the end.

The U.S. government has warned that there is an insurgency in Mexico that is led by drug trafficking cartels, which could potentially take over the government; this would require a military response by the United States, as the strength of Mexico's military and police is limited and inadequate. Here, there's a double game of discourse and practice, formal and informal, in which internal thinking is made explicit and then retracted to respect the protocol of bilateral relations. For public purposes, discourse functions as geopolitical pressure. In the meantime, different government agencies pursue their own agendas.

The U.S. has demanded that Mexico open up a new front in the war on drug trafficking on its border with Guatemala: in this zone, currently dominated by organized crime, conflicts will increase. Despite the resistance of the Mexican government to opening up another front in the south, it's foreseeable that Mexico's defensive role will be reconsidered in terms of its southern border with Central America.[27] The region's weakness demands Mexico's support.

Since 1959, nearly all U.S. wars have been induced and initiated by the country's war machine under the cover of a response to an alleged enemy aggression: a deception and manipulation of important events, often involving the global drug trade.[28] The CIA has carried out illegal operations on a large scale, such as the globalization of torture, selective assassinations and other abuses committed in clandestine prisons,[29] and tends to encourage the internal instability of other nations in order to promote the immediate or future interests of the United States, whether for reasons of domination or influence or to exploit their natural resources. Such is the case with Mexican oil and natural gas, which are abundant in the Gulf of Mexico, as well as several inland areas of the country's north. Or uranium: there are over 50 uranium deposits in Chihuahua.

Mexico City's Binational Intelligence Office hosts agents and bureaucrats from the Pentagon, the CIA, the FBI and the Bureau of Alcohol, Tobacco, Firearms and Explosives (ATF), as well as the Department of Justice, the Department of Homeland Security and the U.S. Treasury. The Pentagon operates through the Defense Intelligence Agency, the National Reconnaissance Office and the National Security Agency; the Department of

Homeland Security through its Coast Guard Intelligence and Immigration and Customs Enforcement agents; the Treasury Department through agents from the Office of Terrorism and Financial Affairs.[30] The Binational Intelligence Office also has facilities in Tijuana, Ciudad Juárez and Escobedo.

The problem of drug trafficking and violence in Latin America cannot be reduced to a game of cops and robbers or a criminological affair: it involves economics, politics, society and culture. It demonstrates, above all else, the serious institutional crisis in Latin America. Its urgency extends through the search for a democratic awakening, the gravitational pull of the global economy and the weight of historical inertias and imbalances. In the cracks of the institutions, inefficacy, ineptitude and corruption have flourished. And an economic scheme has been implemented in which a few privileged individuals benefit from the business of illegality and its most cutting danger: impunity for violence and crime, the breakdown of law and justice.

The importance of drug trafficking and its violence is far from being a perception unleashed by the mass media, as suggested by certain magic bullet theories in which the media has the ability to mold public opinion around a single point of view. The extravagant business of illegality has become one of the biggest threats in Latin America, as it perpetuates itself through the economic and political powers that benefit from it. Governments fight or pretend to fight organized crime while their bureaucracies and security forces are corrupted, all under a hypocritical and manipulative discourse in which there is no longer any connection between words and deeds.

If we have seen anything in the modernization of Latin America over the past two and a half decades, it has been the ineptness of the ruling class in mitigating the asymmetries between democratic norms and the poverty and inequality of their countries: in theory, political alternation and more or less monitored elections would lay the basis for continuous development. Instead, oligarchies, monopolies and rapacious corporations have prevailed, contrary to all egalitarian principles.

The United Nations issued a report in 2008 emphasizing the vulnerability of these countries to crime, particularly drug trafficking, which it says is "the most amenable to collective action."[31] Colombia, Peru and Bolivia produce 1,000 tons of cocaine each year, which reaches at least 10 million users in Europe and the United States through other Latin American countries, creating a situation in which "nearly every country in the hemisphere is affected." The production of cocaine is on the rise, as are seizures of the drug in Venezuela, Trinidad and Tobago, Panama and Costa Rica.

This is due to the troubles of drug traffickers in Colombia, who are relocating their activities into neighboring countries.

Rising cocaine consumption in Europe has increased drug trafficking through West Africa, which has implications for Venezuela and other countries of the southern Caribbean. Despite falling cocaine consumption in the United States, its market remains the largest. In terms of heroin, the hemisphere meets its demand, with Colombia and Mexico serving as the suppliers to slightly over one million addicts. Cannabis consumption, in turn, is "universal," with each country generally supplying its own market, though Paraguay, Colombia and Jamaica are major exporters of this drug to other countries in the region.

This report also emphasizes that the production of methamphetamine to supply U.S. demand was at first overwhelmingly domestic, but has extended first into Mexico and then further south. The Office on Drugs and Crime has warned that the drug trade can fuel other forms of crime, even insurgency, as exemplified by Colombia and, more recently, Mexico. In general, drug trafficking is inseparable from Latin America's rising violence. If drug trafficking seems to be everywhere, it's because it is ubiquitous in society, expanding through spaces created by the institutions themselves. The case of Mexico is currently the most visible at the international level, even though its government denies the seriousness of the problem.

This context explains the growth of the type of criminal organizations exemplified by Central American gangs such as La Mara Salvatrucha and its subculture of glorifying crime. The report emphasizes money laundering and corruption as additional factors that can undermine both the economy and governance. It also mentions that, for example, cannabis consumption is on the rise in Latin America, above all in Argentina, Uruguay, Paraguay, Peru, Venezuela, Jamaica, the Dominican Republic, Honduras and Mexico. And it warns that drug trafficking is just one of the many forms of crime facing the region, and that no country in Latin America is free of the trade in controlled substances. While drug-related violence may be diffused throughout a large population in consumer countries, it concentrates at bottlenecks: zones, routes and critical points used by traffickers. This violence, the report concludes, is not just another form of social conflict, but is instead the result of a vicious cycle: weak law enforcement enables drug trafficking, which, in turn, undermines the rule of law even further.

The production of opium and marijuana have been on the decline in Mexico since 2010, while the fight against cocaine trafficking has intensified and methamphetamine production has expanded.[32] The direction being taken in the fight against drug trafficking in Latin America consists of optimizing control and surveillance.

In 2012, it was announced that the U.S. government uses drones and blimps along the Mexican border to track drug traffickers. Mexico's Navy Secretariat, in turn, revealed its own tactical drone program, used for surveillance and espionage in the fight against organized crime.[33] Nevertheless, Mexico's politicians have not confronted the most serious consequence of this problem: they sidestep the issue of U.S. drone operations along the border or within Mexican territory, as well as the threat that this military technology poses to human rights, which would imply restrictions on the use and retention of images, the obligation to make the use of this technology public and allowing for democratic observation, control and auditing. According to international human rights organizations, the use of drones allows for extrajudicial executions, in violation of international law and human rights statutes, under the theory of the global war on terrorism.[34]

Minimizing problems now and into the future means choosing the path of lies and failure; its consequence will be to facilitate the perpetuation of the war machine and its counterpart, the criminal machine.

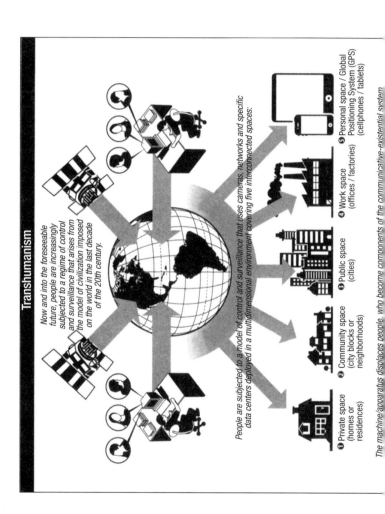

Transhumanism

Now and into the foreseeable future, people are increasingly subjected to a regime of control and surveillance that arises from the model of civilization imposed on the world in the last decade of the 20th century.

People are subjected to a model of control and surveillance that uses cameras, networks and specific data centers deployed in a multidimensional environment covering five interconnected spaces:

❶ Private space (homes or residences)

❷ Community space (city blocks or neighborhoods)

❸ Public space (cities)

❹ Work space (offices / factories)

❺ Personal space / Global Positioning System (GPS) (cellphones / tablets)

The machine/apparatus displaces people, who become components of the communicative-existential system

Epilogue

PLANETARY TRANSHUMANISM

The era of planetary transhumanism is characterized by the incorporation of human beings into a vast military-technological system that allows the species to transcend the conventional biological and social limitations that have restrained it for thousands of years. The transhumanist project is no longer based on aspirations towards collective welfare, but towards the supremacy of those who possess and administer it. The dangers are clear: nation-states are increasingly unable to comprehend the great transformation concealed in the control and surveillance model through the strategy of supplanting the presence of the person (the legal subject par excellence) with the growing hegemony of the two-headed god of money and technique, the axis of a future world programmed through electronic devices.[1]

Now and into the foreseeable future, people are increasingly subjected to a regime of control and surveillance that arises from the model of civilization imposed on the world in the last decade of the 20th century. This model configures the type of citizen of the emerging order, which combines ultraliberalism, the globalized economy, formal or procedural democracy, corporate practices that transcend the nation-state, telecommunications and technological advances sparked by the revolution in military affairs.

This model not only includes military domination through the multilateral operations carried out under the unified command of the United States,[2] but also the search for a common regulatory framework for politics, economics, security and the environment through a variety of international institutions. The one-world logic brings together environmental, economic, technological and consumption priorities in a utopia for all in the here and now that arises from shared norms: science, logical reasoning, the free market economy, individualization, a social contract that establishes responsibilities for both the rulers and the ruled and multilateralism in international affairs. Norms that validate themselves as the dogmas of a secular faith.[3] The "new world order": government and culture are unanimous, managed by supranational military, corporate and financial elites and the mob of bureaucrats and servants who defend the myths of endless economic growth as a universal panacea, the extermination of natural and energy resources, the exploitation of people in both work and leisure, the attack on the sovereignty of the nation-state, etc.

To achieve one world, people need to be subjected to a model of control and surveillance that uses cameras, networks and specific data centers deployed in a multidimensional environment covering five interconnected spaces: 1) private space (homes or residences), 2) community space (neighborhoods, churches, clubs, gyms, parks), 3) public space (streets, avenues, public plazas, building lobbies, places for leisure and relaxation, sports facilities, cultural centers, theaters, shopping malls, transit centers, airports, government offices, police stations), 4) work space (factories, offices, warehouses); 5) personal space (journeys by land, air and sea, temporary lodgings, places of rest: the full-time availability provided by the global positioning systems contained in portable electronic devices). The ideal of the panopticon that aspires to see all has mutated into the oligopticon: those who see best.[4]

The cosmopolitan citizen and their simultaneous experience of "contradictory identities and loyalties"[5] will be eclipsed by the citizen connected to a unit or singularity within "systems of systems" or ultracontemporary networks.[6] It is alleged that the control and surveillance model is applied neutrally, being equally available to the economic and political powers as to any private individual. To justify itself, this argument necessarily overlooks the origins, functions and uses of telecommunications, particularly the central role of the military perspective on civilian life in the emerging model of the global order. It's therefore important to analyze U.S. espionage programs, such as Prism and XKeyscore, which have also been imitated in other countries.[7]

In 2012, the U.S. National Security Council published a report on global trends looking forward to the year 2030.[8] This council is an administrative agency answering to the president that concerns itself with foreign policy and national security; its members include the vice president, the secretary of state, the secretary of defense and the national security advisor. Its research takes into consideration both the continuity of the existent as well as the emergence of new possibilities at the global level, predicting and modeling the future based on contemporary factors and offering results relevant to the interests, capacities and directives of its authors over the medium term.

This report, developed by U.S. academics in collaboration with experts from around the world, proposes a "framework" for thinking about the future. Its method distinguishes between "megatrends," which will likely occur under any scenario, and "game-changers," critical variables whose trajectories are far less certain. The diversity and complexity of many emergent factors makes it imperative to pay close attention to each alternate scenario or world that may come to pass. There are four megatrends: a) the empowerment of individuals or small groups (due to poverty reduction, the growth of the global middle class, greater educational attainment and health care advances); b) the diffusion of hegemonic power and the emergence of networks and coalitions in a multipolar world; c) demographic patterns (the demographic arc of instability will narrow and economic growth may decline in aging countries—a process that is already underway in Mexico and Spain, for example—while 60% of the world's population will live in cities and migration will increase); d) the food, water and energy nexus (access to each of these resources will be subject to the supply and demand for the others).

The report also lists six game-changers: a) a crisis-prone global economy (volatility, imbalance and differing interests that could either provoke a collapse or, due to greater multipolarity, lead to increased resilience); b) the governance gap (the possibility of either harnessing change or being overwhelmed by it); c) the potential for increased conflict (rapid changes and shifts in power could lead to more intrastate and interstate conflicts); d) a wider scope of regional instability (in the Middle

East or South Asia, for example) that could spill over and create global insecurity; e) the impact of new technologies; f) the role of the United States (it must seek out new partners to reinvent the international system).

In terms of potential worlds, the report considers four possibilities: a) stalled engines (the U.S. draws inward and globalization stalls); b) fusion (global cooperation on a range of issues, for example between the U.S. and China); c) Gini-out-of-the-bottle (runaway inequality leads to increasing social tensions and, without completely disengaging, the U.S. is no longer the "global policeman"); d) a non-state world (driven by new technologies, non-state actors take the lead in confronting global challenges).

It is interesting to compare the National Security Council's report with Joint Vision 2020, a strategy plan for the U.S. Armed Forces. The former has a civilian focus with a military substrate that goes unmentioned in the report itself, while in the latter, as should be obvious, the military perspective predominates.

The supremacy of the United States at the end of the 20th century and the beginning of the 21st is due to its military power. This power is derived from technological transformations that are applied to operations defending the national

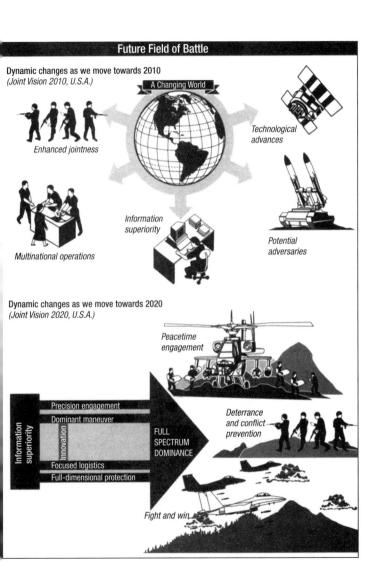

Future Field of Battle

Dynamic changes as we move towards 2010
(Joint Vision 2010, U.S.A.)

A Changing World

Enhanced jointness

Technological advances

Multinational operations

Information superiority

Potential adversaries

Dynamic changes as we move towards 2020
(Joint Vision 2020, U.S.A.)

Peacetime engagement

Information superiority

Precision engagement
Dominant maneuver
Innovation
Focused logistics
Full-dimensional protection

FULL SPECTRUM DOMINANCE

Deterrance and conflict prevention

Fight and win

interests and global responsibilities of the United States and its allies, as well as those combating persistent threats and future challenges. If the Joint Vision 2010 strategy plan emphasized the military transition from the industrial age to the information age, Joint Vision 2020[9] deals with the maneuver, strike, logistics and protection aspects of full spectrum dominance to ensure flexibility and responsiveness.

The mandate of the armed forces consists of being persuasive in peacetime and decisive in times of war. Its strategic evolution is influenced by two factors: the development and proliferation of information technologies that will shape the conduct of military operations (in which information is the basis of superiority) and the intellectual and technical innovations that fuel changes in the strategic environment. Accordingly, the United States will engage with a variety of regional actors: "Transportation, communications, and information technology will continue to evolve and foster expanded economic ties and awareness of international events."[10] Security, economic interests and political values provide the impetus for engagement with international partners through operations involving multinational forces and the coordination of said operations with government agencies and international institutions. The U.S. Army also reserves the right to act through contractors.[11]

This strategic context allows potential adversaries to access much of the same technology as the U.S. military through global trade, and so superiority must be guaranteed less from technological advantage and more from leaders, personnel, doctrines, organization and proper training. In this competitive situation, superiority must go beyond dominance through conventional military means and confront the problem of asymmetrical warfare: the interaction between one strong actor and one or several weak actor(s).

Joint Vision 2020's plan for full spectrum dominance takes five sources of friction into consideration: 1) the effects of danger and exertion; 2) the existence of uncertainty and chance; 3) the unpredictable actions of other actors; 4) the frailties of machines and information; 5) human frailties. The response to these sources of friction lies in flexibility and adaptation to change. Just as in antiquity, this strategic plan recognizes that information is the key to ensuring victory. The concept of information superiority is defined as "the capability to collect, process, and disseminate an uninterrupted flow of information while exploiting or denying an adversary's ability to do the same."[12]

Multinational corporations engage in analogous strategic exercises.[13] In military strategy, informational superiority derives from the individuals, organizations and systems that collect, process or disseminate information. The variables of informational operations include the multidimensional definition and meaning of information (target, weapon, resource or domain of operations), the level of action or desired effect (tactical, operational, strategic or some combination thereof), the objective of the operation (providing information, perception management, battlefield dominance, command and control warfare, systemic disruption or systemic destruction) and, finally, the nature of the situation (peace, crisis or conflict). Assessing means and ends requires a global information environment (sea, air, land, space and cyberspace).

The Joint Vision 2020 strategy plan can be read as a system of systems due to its demand for interoperability, which is the ability of systems, units or forces to provide and accept services from other systems, units or forces and to use the services so exchanged to enable them to operate effectively together. The desired results require commanders and teams that understand new operational capabilities and support tools—often highly automated—in order to be capable of flexible, adaptive coordination and direction, utilizing up-to-date knowledge of the battlefield and coordinating small, agile, dispersed, interacting and networked units, resulting in plural, simultaneous operations. This joint force seeks to establish compatible, interoperable multinational agencies utilizing shared information. A prospect of experience and innovation built on a foundation shared with the business sector: the world as a field of opportunities for profit, a field of real or virtual war.

Both the National Security Council report and the Joint Vision 2020 strategy plan emphasize the supremacy of the United States in the global future, albeit with differences in form and degree. They also both recognize the importance of technology, especially to the extent that it handles information and information products. If the report avoids an explicit statement of the decisive role of control and surveillance for military and civilian life now and in the coming decades, the strategy plan describes their great future utility: "The evolution of information technology will increasingly permit us to integrate the traditional forms of information operations with sophisticated all-source intelligence, surveillance, and reconnaissance in a fully synchronized information campaign." An interconnected global network for managing and providing "information on demand to warfighters, policymakers, and support personnel."[14] In turn, the "technological assets" mentioned in the National Security Council report indicate the juncture between military and civilian life: people, their behavior and their consumption habits are monitored over the Internet and other platforms.[15]

The 2013 revelations of the worldwide surveillance by the U.S. government of the communications of citizens, actual or potential criminals, governments, "friends" and allies demonstrates the seriousness of these attacks on the rights and freedoms of individuals.

One of the notable differences between traditional methods of control and surveillance and their ultracontemporary manifestations is the transition from analog storage devices (paper, for example) to electronic storage. The implications of this are wide-ranging and profound. A comparative analysis[16] of traditional and emergent methods of control and surveillance indicates that the latter utilize the artificial extension of the senses, can be either visible or invisible, tend to lack the consent of the observed, are cheaper than traditional methods and are almost always remote and undetectable. Data collection becomes automatized and information is immediately transmitted to an interconnected network that is shared among various agencies and is temporally continuous, uniting the past, present and future in a virtual environment, with its data always available in "real time."

The technological assets used for ultracontemporary control and surveillance are available on the open market, which contributes to the illusion that they are a neutral technology and that specific data is instantly assimilated into complex processes that exceed individual comprehension.

In the emerging model of control and surveillance, information is entered into data banks that tend to decontextualize it under an apparently neutral utility, while its scope and penetration increase, as the possession of data provides knowledge lacked by each person, who becomes an anonymous entity. This constructs a set of persons: an informational mass. Converted into a number, each person-entity or unit is connected to a network that is in turn connected to other networks. Data and person-entities are subjected to the manipulation of reality and the effects of simulation, when records are audiovisual and divisible.

Information is analyzed by experts in a dispersed, impersonal, self-monitoring network. Data can be efficiently obtained, handled, stored, recovered and analyzed using a combination of methods (visually, textually, aurally, digitally) and the transmission and reception of this information is easier than with traditional methods, when records were kept on paper. Big Data.

The ethical criteria used to confront this control and surveillance must take into consideration how data collection can avoid harming individuals, the validity or invalidity of the data in question, privacy

and informed consent, as well as practical limitations, public discussion of standards and periodic,
systematic inspection and revision of procedures,
among other aspects.[17] The same should be considered for the use of the information collected and
to be collected. Each country, in accordance with
international treaties and norms, should guarantee
the defense of individual rights.

And if individuals are those who should receive
the first priority in terms of protection from the
abuses and excesses of states, corporations and the
unilateral and joint actions of armed forces, then
urban areas, where the majority of the world's
population resides, should also limit control and
surveillance, denouncing and pushing back against
the vision that reduces cities to a real or potential
field of battle in which individuals can become
operational targets at any time.

The idea of control and surveillance within and
beyond the nation-state brings with it a logic that
encompasses popular culture, industrial production, war and the design of autonomous and
human-operated weapons systems.[18] And it also
implies a technophilic ideology based around a
phobia of difference that is opposed to urbanity
and turns on the other, which is objectified as a
target of the violence of the powerful: the new
militarized urbanism, which has been in development for years in places such as airport facilities

and has recently been applied to city streets and crowd control.[19]

To resist this, political action and pacifist solutions become imperative; we must question the rise of the global "securitocracy," fundamentalist positions, the connection between war and entertainment and the increasing turn to states of "emergency" or "exception" or the "law of the enemy" (or law outside the law).[20] It's essential to restore a substantive legality, a sense of limits and a defense of difference as part of an equitable geography and a democratic understanding of urban space and the public and the private.

To counter the permanence of zones under surveillance, which are subject to the hierarchization of urban power under centralized, transnational networks, other practices must arise that are more dispersed, allowing and encouraging the participation of people outside their predestined roles (leisure, political clientelism, consumption, mediatic and transmediatic fear). In particular, the invisible foundations of these practices must be made visible and there must be a public discussion on military interventions in urban space, their coercive, violent mandate and the privileges of the powerful that are favored by such a strategy. These policies must be emphasized so that art, social activism or alternate applications of cartography can be used to denounce, contain and resist the militarist vision and its imperial extensions into civilian life. And to generally break with the military-police logic, which dictates that "you're either with us or against us" and imposes a Manichean world with only two sides: us or them.[21]

An alternate vision has been proposed, one based around solidarity, fluidity, egalitarianism and community control. This would involve collaboration at the global level to eradicate the militarization of control and surveillance and institute other practices in society, politics, the media and culture that favor pluralistic coexistence over binary thinking, the manipulation of information and opacity.[22] Furthermore, a critique of political economy must be undertaken in order to examine the asymmetries of the global order and transform our ultracontemporary reality.

A 2006 report on the future, prepared by the UN in conjunction with other international agencies,[23] argued that the evolution of world history points to a world government with a globalized economy and online communication. Its pacifist focus hides the military factor that has stimulated both economic development and the technological revolution in everyday life, from the dawn of modernity up until the present. It defends a position of peace and collective collaboration in the future, in which one of three possible scenarios will prevail: 1) conventional worlds, in which "market forces" and "policy reform" will prevail; 2) barbarization, which foresees a total societal breakdown or the institution of a fortress world (this can be identified with the militarist vision, the "securitocracy" of control and surveillance); 3) great transitions, which consists of "eco-communalism" and a "new sustainability paradigm" (solidarity and new values such as peace, freedom, development and environmentalism), which would be achieved around 2068.

In this scenario, by 2025, or a little over a decade from now, a network of Value-Based Organizations (VBOs) dedicated to action will secure "the globalization of civil society" through the use of communication platforms. The report offers a fictitious history of the near future: "Global networks of VBO's, armed with digital cameras and other sensors, proved to be the ideal counterforce to predatory global corporations and incompetent governments. They organized vast networks to monitor corporate behavior—how and where they logged forests, the quality of their working conditions and wages, and their contributions to local communities. The information was posted on the Internet, often with video footage. They pressured retailers to shun offending companies and consumers to boycott their products. The VBO networks brought powerful market pressures on global companies. Governments who failed to provide basic services to the poor, to protect environmentally sensitive resources or to uphold universal rights, were the objects of equally powerful political pressures. By enforcing transparency and demanding accountability, these bottom-up networks of activist citizens provided a rapid and powerful social feedback mechanism, far more potent than formal regulatory efforts of governments and intergovernmental bodies."

This futurist report, released before the global economic crisis of 2008, before the rise of groups such as Anonymous and WikiLeaks and before the leaks from within espionage agencies, contained a diagnostic of history and the present that seemed plausible at the time, but now seems precarious in 2013. Online activism has, to date, shown itself to be particularly limited and ineffective in the face of military power, corporate interests and the policies of nation-states. Securing meaningful advances towards a radical change in human consciousness requires much more than faith in new information and communications technologies. Above all, we need an understanding and critique of reality, its inertias and its functioning on a deeper level than that provided by evolutionary technocratic pacifism.

In the case of the European Union, the Project Europe 2030 report (published in 2010) recognizes the instability of the present and predicts that, over the next 20 years, "there will not only be several poles of power, but the world's centre of gravity will also have shifted—to Asia and the global south, to new public and private actors, upwards to transnational institutions."[24] The central challenge consists of facing this transformation, whose dynamism conditions the energy supply (fossil fuels, which largely have to be imported, with a complement of renewable energy) under the threat of climate change.

Project Europe 2030's model is a highly competitive "social market economy" that aims to generate growth and jobs, along with selective social investments: a new deal creating a single market across the continent and economic governance in the interest of stability and union. To the above, the report adds environmental sustainability, improvements to the education system, increased spending on research and development, a new regulatory framework designed to unleash innovation and creativity, demographic rationality and effective immigration policies. It also alludes to external security and controls on illegal immigration.

Against the technological-military trend of control and surveillance, Project Europe 2030 proposes developing and maintaining a "space of freedom, security and justice," arguing that "we now need to take decisive action and implement a new

'European Security Model.'" This model draws on the vision and objectives of the then-recently-adopted Internal Security Strategy (2010) to "prioritise the interests of European citizens while addressing the rapidly evolving challenges of the 21st century."[25] This report prescribes protecting individual rights and freedoms, improving cooperation and solidarity between member states and addressing the causes of insecurity instead of just its effects. To achieve these goals, it recommends prioritizing prevention and citizen engagement and recognizing the interdependence between the internal and external dimensions of security through the establishment of a "global security" approach with other countries.

In the military sphere, Project Europe 2030 acknowledges the shortfalls of European Union member countries, especially when compared to the United States. Europe's total military spending is about half the U.S. military budget, while its overseas force projecting capabilities amount to only 10–15 % of U.S. capabilities. The European Union accepts that there is insufficient investment in the type of capabilities needed to respond to new security situations (rapid deployment forces, strategic air transport, helicopters, communications, military police): "with 1.8 million soldiers under arms—half a million more than the US— the EU is not capable of deploying a 60,000-strong rapid intervention force and it finds it hard to deliver a 5,000-strong force for a Common Security and Defence Policy (CSDP) mission."[26] Seventy percent of European land forces are unfit for overseas operations, despite the fact that emerging conflicts require deployable and sustainable expeditionary forces. In general, European CSDP missions tend to be piecemeal and forced by exigencies rather than responding to an overarching strategy or plan. This is largely due to the fact that the EU has no common funding for its missions: with no fair burden-sharing among member states, there are disincentives to participating in military missions, and in terms of the arms market, "it costs Europe much more to produce far fewer products than other arms suppliers like the US": the paradigm for the future.

The conclusion of Project Europe 2030 makes its position on the military optimization of the European Union clear: "The EU needs to agree on a long-term vision of EU defence, which could be laid out in a White Paper with clearly defined priorities in terms of threats, engagement criteria and earmarked resources."[27] The strength of member states demands superior military performance than that seen today.

The civil focus and defense of individual rights and freedoms seen in Project Europe 2030 concurs with the European Parliament's Report on a New

Digital Agenda for Europe 2015, whose focus on a "prosperous and competitive economy" defends accessibility, transparency, equality, pluralism and privacy in information and communications technology, above all because Europe is "the 'mobile continent' in the world," where "75% of mobile subscribers are mobile broadband users with access to high-speed wireless services."[28] At the dawn of the second decade of the 21st century, for example, Spain led Europe in the sale of mobile devices, which were primarily used for entertainment, with literacy falling by the wayside.[29] By overlooking the risks of control and surveillance, ultracontemporary technophilia contributes to transhumanism and the militarization of civil society.

On the issue of control and surveillance, the European Parliament seems to put too much trust in provisions on net "neutrality" and services provided by transnational corporations who have, in recent years, shown their invasive reach in monitoring the production, circulation and consumption patterns of individuals.[30] Given this context, it's significant that the U.S. Total Information Awareness program, which is based on millions of surveillance cameras and interlocking computer networks and systems, is already in operation in one European country: the United Kingdom.[31] This pioneering application has become decisive for the rest of Europe.

A study of the wars of the second half of the 20th century will reveal that their determining factors were ethnicity and violence as a consequence of polarization and fragmentation, which arose from issues in which politics intersects with economics. The instrumentation of interests and benefits thus becomes more important than the hatreds themselves.[32] Both the potential for antagonism and the future possibility of constructing models for understanding this implacable process remain open.

The search for alternate solutions involving individual and collective participation, in order to transform the existing order, oscillates between pacifist and insurrectionist thought. One example of the transnational and ecumenical ideology of nonviolence can be found in groups such as L'Arche de Saint-Antoine, which argues that, "Those who renounce violence have no defense. When properly trained and disciplined, they can form a strong nonviolent civil defense force. This can be defined as the struggle of an entire people to stop evil and neutralize the enemy with methods that respect life and others, leaving open an opportunity for dialogue. This force has nothing to do with wealth or privilege and cannot be monopolized by the government. Women participate to the same extent as men. Nonviolence arises from the righteousness of the cause and the unity of all those who struggle. The means are therefore consistent with the end

Person and Insurrection

Individual Rights and Freedoms

Ethical Dilemma

when nonviolence is used. With weapons, it is the end that justifies the means. Furthermore, weapons, especially weapons of mass destruction, are invented to destroy the values we wish to protect. The power of the truth makes us conscious of injustice and of our responsibilities."[33] Pacifism is confident that it will triumph in the 21st century.

One year before the great economic crisis of 2008, a manifesto was published[34] that not only predicted the collapse of the world's financial system, but also advocated for an imminent insurrection at the global level. Its communitarian impulse called on the multitude to organize itself, starting by training, learning and discussing reality and its hardships. It also proposed creating shared territories of inconformity and insurrectionary activism with "zones of opacity" for the conventional powers, opening up lines of communication with other communities and territories in rebellion around the world, bringing systematic insurrection to other regions, overcoming obstacles one by one, adopting an anonymous identity and making organizations invisible, as well as organizing for self-defense, making the most of every crisis, sabotaging representative authorities, blocking the economy, liberating territories from police occupation, deposing authorities at the local level and avoiding the use of arms whenever possible, instead privileging new political practices. Without explicitly saying so, this manifesto expressed a theory of asymmetrical force.

Both pacifism and insurrectionary movements tend to converge in their use of solutions that exploit the asymmetric nature of their "weakness" in the face of hegemonic powers. In traditional terms, this asymmetry is 1:2.

In contemporary assessments, the following formulation is used: "A conflict (is) coded asymmetric if the halved product of one actor's armed forces and population exceed(s) the simple product of its adversary's armed forces and population by 5:1 or more."[35] The study of the asymmetries of conflicts has led to the following formulation: the greater the power gap, the less resolute and therefore more politically vulnerable strong actors will be, while weak actors are more resolute and less politically vulnerable. Consequently, to predict the results of an asymmetrical conflict, the strategic interactions between actors should be observed.

For example, the best outcome for a weak actor would result from a direct attack (targeting the enemy's capacity to wage war) against an indirect defense (targeting the enemy's will to continue the attack); the second best outcome for a weak actor would be from an indirect attack (targeting the enemy's will to wage war) against an indirect defense (targeting the enemy's will to continue the attack).[36] This would explain the military difficulties of the United States in Vietnam, Somalia, Iraq and Afghanistan.

It seems contradictory to apply pacifist thought to the field of battle. Nevertheless, its language and practices speak of peace as a weapon for waging war.[37] These doctrinal adaptations lead us to think that, in the future, the situation facing humanity will not be one of the party of war versus the party of peace, but of a generalized clash between two distinct methods of waging war within a single system.

The future is nonexistent without the present moment, which is almost entirely at odds with the prescriptions for progress that tend to be given. There's a disproportionate asymmetry between present reality and the desire for transformation. Trends and inertias force us to develop another approach. Perhaps, by studying the asymmetries of the economy, politics, society and culture, we can find a reserve of unexplored dreams of the future: asymmetries, anomalies and differences are also transformative principles that could resist techno-logical-military transhumanism.

The economic and political integration of the world sees the asymmetries between countries as a permanent threat, and has occasionally been able to capitalize on this. The Treaty on European Union (TEU) entered into force in 1993; the North American Free Trade Agreement (NAFTA) followed one year later. The geopolitical context at the time was the revolution in military affairs launched by the United States, which has guided the course of globalization ever since. Twenty years later, the U.S. Department of Defense has urged that, despite all the practical limitations involved, Europe and the North Atlantic Treaty Organization (NATO) should join it in its pivot towards the new security focus of the 21st century and its looming threats: the vast territory of Asia and the Pacific.[38]

The case of Mexico and its economic, political and military integration with the interests of the United States shows how it has been possible to take advantage of asymmetry, the alegality of a state and the imposition of comprehensive reforms of a country's production, intelligence, penal and security systems in order to appropriate them, little by little, in accordance with the needs of the United States in the 21st century. Mexico's years of extreme violence and instability have played their role in all this, disrupting the country's real and symbolic space through emerging cartographies that are adverse for the majority of its population.

The results of this appropriative process reveal a society in crisis, with few hopes for the future, which need to be reformulated. This case can serve as a warning for other parts of the world and help bring about ways of confronting what is to come, particularly in terms of resisting the military approach based around technology and the control and surveillance of individuals, who are seen as mere units subjected to a superindividual order controlled by powers that are increasingly concentrated and unassailable. A world divided between director-analysts and person-entities, actors and their life world far removed from the ideals of education, welfare and culture, instead immersed in consumption and entertainment. The great mass seeks to learn the skills needed for the ultra-connected systems and devices that dominate labor and private life, and that determine individual spending (community violence, leisure, narcosis, sexuality, etc.), but ignore the dangers of extreme neglect. Social malaise has become malleable, virtually a living anamorphosis under the abuses and omissions of the constituted power and the depredations of criminal power.

Humanity has never known so much about nature and the structure of the cosmos as it does now, and never has it been so far from the stars. Fortunately, the future remains a mystery.

Drones for Control and Surveillance

Notes

Preface: The Notion of a Field

1. For a military reading of the terms flattening or smoothness: Shimon Naveh, "Between the Striated and the Smooth," *Cabinet Magazine*, Issue 22, Summer 2006: http://www.cabinet-magazine. org/issues/22/naveh.php; the geopolitical, cultural and economic ideology behind these terms is in: Thomas L. Friedman, *The World is Flat 3.0, A Brief History of the Twenty-First Century*, New York, Picador, 2007, 660 pp.

2. Prohibitionism is rooted in the Puritan/Anglo-Saxon faith and has given rise to a strategy of geopolitical defense: prohibition= war versus liberalization=terrorism. Cf. Daniel L. Whitten, "Perspective on the Military Involvement in the War on Drugs— Is There a Better Way?," Alabama, Air University, 1999, 39 pp.

3. And the field, at the extreme, is the space that opens up when the state of exception becomes a rule: Giorgio Agamben, "¿Qué es un campo?" in *Medios sin fin*, Valencia, Pre-Textos, 2010, 121 pp. Pierre Bourdieu, *Campo de poder, campo intelectual. Itinerario de un concepto*, Buenos Aires, Montressor, 2002, 127 pp.: http://es.scribd.com/doc/4799565/bourdieu-pierre-campo-de -poder-campo-intelectual; also: https://es.wikipedia.org/wiki /Campo_(sociologia). The basis of Sun Tzu's strategic thinking is based around "knowing the place" of the coming battle, the field of virtual advantages that make the difference between life and death. Cf. Sun Tzu, *The Art of War*, North Clarendon, Vermont, Tuttle Publishing, 1996, 128 pp.

4. A study of the continental geopolitics of the United States can be found in Josué Ángel González Torres, "Control hemisférico de los Estados Unidos: El Comando Norte": http://www.tuobra.unam.mx/vistaObra.html?obra=3303.

5. Latour's proposal to abandon the concept of the panopticon for that of the oligopticon is key for understanding the control and surveillance model to be applied in the future. See Bruno Latour, *Re-ensamblar lo social. Una introducción a la teoría del actor-red.* Buenos Aires, Manantial, 2008, pp.178–186.

1. Postnational Map

1. The 1994 neo-indigenist uprising against the state in southeastern Mexico sparked the period of anti-institutional actions that would culminate in the rise of organized crime at the beginning of the 21st century. The characteristics of these guerrillas and their social networks express the emergent forms of future warfare: fourth generation warfare. Cf. John Arquilla and David Ronfelt, *Networks and Netwars: The Future of Terror, Crime and Militancy,* Santa Monica (CA), Rand Corporation, 2001, 352 pp.

2. The myth of American abundance and the reduction of the Earth to a mere source of material resources extends from the colonial to the postcolonial era. Cf. Irma Beatriz García Rojas, "El cuerno de la abundancia: mito e identidad en el discurso sobre el territorio y la nación mexicana," *Revue Histoire(s) de l'Amerique Latine,* vol. 2005, pp. 1–25. Also: http://www.hisal.org/index.php?journal=revue&page=article&op=view&path%5b%5d=2005-9.

3. In 2011, the U.S.A. controlled 78% of the world's arms market: Tom Englehardt, "The Pentagon: A Global NRA," The Nation, January 14, 2013: http://www.thenation.com/article/172194/pentagon-global-nra.

The American arms industry provides armament for itself and others: EFE, "EU es el mayor exportador de armas en el mundo," March 19, 2012: http://www.vanguardia.com.mx/eueselmayorexportadordearmasenelmundo-1243904.html; "7 de cada 10 armas usadas por criminales en México viene de EU: ATF," April 27, 2012, Animal Político: http://www.animalpolitico.com/2012/04/7-de-cada-10-armas-usadas-por-criminales-en-mexico-vienen

-de-eu-atf/. Also, Magda Coss Nogueda, *El tráfico de armas en México,* Mexico, Grijalbo, 2011, 199 pp.

4. The triumph of Anglo-Saxon capitalism in modernity imposes the economistic perspective and the strategy of maximum production, which begins with the sense, use, surveillance and control of available space for domination and exploitation. See Karl Schlögel, *En el espacio leemos el tiempo. Sobre historia de la civilización y geopolítica*, Madrid, Siruela, 2007, p. 246.

5. The objectification/subjectification of the territory and maps in military situations evokes the subjective maps conceived by the avant-garde over the course of the 20th century, from surrealism to situationism. Cf. Estrella de Diego, *Contra el mapa*, Madrid, Siruela, 2008, 103 pp.

6. On the collective imaginaries that are the product of the territorial influence and dominance of organized crime and its exploitation of migrants traveling to the United States from Central America, cf. Óscar Martínez, *Los migrantes que no cuentan*, Mexico, El Faro/Sur+, 2012, 291 pp.

7. The numbers of those displaced by the war on drug trafficking oscillates between 239,000 people and 1.6 million people. This displacement modifies the population map, which is never the same after any military or criminal action. Cf. "239 mil desplazados por la guerra contra el narco," Animal Político, March 29, 2011: http://www.animalpolitico.com/2011/03/239-mil-desplazados -por-la-guerra-contra-el-narco/; Gloria Leticia Díaz, "Desplazados 1,6 millones de mexicanos por guerra contra el crimen organiza-do," *Proceso*, November 28, 2011. Also: http://www.proceso.com. mx/?p=289550.

8. Comisión Nacional de Derechos Humanos, Comunicado 185, 15/12/2008; also Liliana Alcántara, "Ve CNDH impunidad en 99 por ciento de los delitos," *El Universal*, December 15, 2008: http://www.eluniversal.com.mx/nacion/164447.html. In 2013, this impunity rate has not declined in any meaningful way. Also the report, *Elementos para la construcción de una política de Estado para la seguridad y la justicia en democracia*, Mexico, UNAM/IIDC, 2011, 39 pp. Also, Diana Bautista, "Dejan

impunes 93% de los delitos," *Reforma*, December 29, 2013: http://www.reforma.com/nacional/articulo/726/1450383/default .asp?PlazaConsulta=reforma&DirCobertura&TipoCob=0.

9. The National Human Rights Commission (CNDH) has recorded 77 assassinations of journalists between 2000 and April 2012: http://www.animalpolitico.com/2012/04/cndh-tiene-registrados -76-asesinatos-de-comunicadores-desde-el-2000/.

10. Luigi Ferrajoli, *Poderes salvajes. La crisis de la democracia constitucional.* Madrid, Trotta, 2011, p. 40.

11. Luigi Ferrajoli, *Garantismo y Derecho penal. Un diálogo con Ferrajoli*, Mexico, Ubijus, 2010, p. 16.

12. Luigi Ferrajoli, "Pasado y futuro del Estado de derecho," in Miguel Carbonell, editor, *Neoconstitucionalismo(s)*, Mexico/Madrid, UNAM/Trotta, 2009, pp. 13–29.

13. *Rule of Law Index*, The Justice Project, Washington, 2011, pp. 26 and 79: http://worldjusticeproject.org/rule-of-law-index. The 2012 evaluation is likewise negative for Mexico: https://worldjusticeproject .org/our-work/wjp-rule-law-index/special-reports/rule-law-mexico.

14. Antonio Baranda, "Queda oculto el 91 por ciento de los delitos," *Reforma*, September 28, 2012.

15. The historic facts of this period are documented in Elaine Shannon, *Desperados: Latin Drug Lords, U.S. Lawmen, and the War America Can't Win*, New York, Viking, 1989, 528 pp.

16. Humberto Padgett, "El Cártel de la DEA," Mexico, *Emeequis*, January 9, 2012, pp. 28–38; Francisco Marín, "La CIA financiada por el narco," *Proceso*, December 3, 2012, pp. 64–67.

17. The information and analysis regarding the role of the CIA in Mexico cited in these pages were provided to the author by a government intelligence consultant, who requested anonymity.

18. Amada María Arley Orduña, *Más allá del TLCAN. ASPAN ¿qué es y a dónde vamos?*, Mexico, Porrúa, 2011, p. 161. In 2002, Mexico's Supreme Court defended the following thesis: "International treaties are hierarchically located below the

Constitution and above general federal and local laws, as per the customs of international law, *pacta sunt servanda*, under which obligations before the international community that have been freely agreed upon may not be breached on the basis of domestic law" (Amparo/120–2002): http://207.249.17.176/Transparencia /Epocas/Segunda%20sala/NOVENA/78.pdf. In 2012, the Chamber of Deputies passed the General Law on the Approval of Treaties with the goal of preventing the president from approving international treaties, such as the SPP and the Mérida Initiative, without the approval of the Senate: "Expiden la Ley General sobre Celebración y Aprobación de Tratados," *Diario Juridico*, April 26, 2012: http://diariojuridico.com.mx/actualidad/noticias/expiden -la-ley-general-sobre-celebracion-y-aprobacion-de-tratados.html.

19. According to the Canadian government's press release, besides ratifying the 2005 agreement, the five priorities in North America in 2006 and 2007 were "strengthening competitiveness in North America; North American Emergency Management; Avian and Pandemic Influenza; North American Energy Security; and North American Smart Secure Borders": "Prime Minister Announces North American Leaders' Summit in Canada," Ottawa, June 15, 2007: https://www.canada.ca/en/news/archive/2007/06/prime -minister-announces-north-american-leaders-summit-canada.html.

20. The U.S. government took its idea of "transformation," also known as the Rumsfeld Doctrine, from the concept of Revolution in Military Affairs: Defense Department, *Transformation Planning Guidance*, U.S.A., April 2003, 39 pp.

21. Ibid, p. 8.

22. "Entrenan mercenarios a soldados en País," *Reforma*, April 6, 2011; Bill Conroy, "U.S. Private Sector Providing Drug-War Mercenaries to Mexico," April 3, 2011, https://narcosphere .narconews.com/notebook/bill-conroy/2011/04/us-private-sector- providing-drug-war-mercenaries-mexico.html.

23. Peter Dale Scott, *American War Machine*, Lanham (Maryland), Rowman & Littlefield Publishers, 2010, 408 pp.; Gary Webb, *Dark Alliance: The CIA, the Contras and the Crack Cocaine Explosion*, New York, Seven Stories Press, 1998, 592 pp.

24. National Security Council, Directive 5412, U.S.A., March 15, 1954: http://history.state.gov/historicaldocuments/frus1964-68v12/actionsstatement.

25. Ernesto Grün, *Una visión sistémica y cibernética del Derecho en el mundo globalizado del siglo XXI*, Mexico, UNAM, 2006, p. 93; *The National Security Strategy of the United States of America*, U.S.A., September 2002, 31 pp.: https://www.state.gov/documents/organization/63562.pdf.

26. Doris Gómora, "El Chapo compró el jet de la CIA," *El Universal*, September 5, 2008: http://www.eluniversal.com.mx/nacion/162152.html; Bill Conroy, "New Document Provides Further Evidence That Owner of Crashed Cocaine Jet Was a U.S. Government Operative," *The Narco News Bulletin*, December 1, 2007: http://www.narconews.com/Issue48/article2919.html.

27. Hannah Stone, "US Targets Bank in Mexico Money Laundering Crackdown," InSight Crime, May 10, 2011: http://www.insightcrime.org/news-analysis/us-targets-bank-in-mexico-money-laundering-crackdown.

28. On the case of General Óscar Naranjo: Carlos Fazio, "Basada en corrupción y mentiras, la historia del colombiano Óscar Naranjo," *La Jornada*, June 30, 2012.

29. Ignacio Alzaga, "Naranjo ve una narco-campaña contra él," *Milenio diario*, September 22, 2012. Lino González Veiguela, "¿Quién es el general Naranjo?, October 3, 2012: http://www.fronterad.com/?q=node/6208. In 2014, Naranjo resigned as advisor to the Mexican government: Inés Santaelulalia, "El general Naranjo deja México," *El País*, January 24, 2014: http://internacional.elpais.com/internacional/2014/01/24/actualidad/1390602323_372282.html.

30. U.S. Senate Permanent Subcommittee on Investigations, "U.S. Vulnerabilities to Money Laundering, Drugs, and Terrorist Financing: HSBC Case History," Washington, U.S. Senate, July 17, 2012, p. 108.

31. Renato Ravelo, "La historia oficial," *Proceso*, March 11, 2007: http://hemeroteca.proceso.com.mx/?page_id=278958&a51dc263 66d99bb5fa29cea4747565fec=94497&rl=wh.

32. Zhenli Ye Gon, "Carta," *El Universal*, July 16, 2007.

33. Francisco Gómez and Francisco Reséndiz, "Obtiene Ye Gon en mandato de Montiel licencia para laboratorio," *El Universal*, August 5, 2007. Ye Gon's laboratory was opened while the governor was Arturo Montiel, the antecessor and uncle of Enrique Peña Nieto, former governor of Mexico State and the president of Mexico since 2012.

34. "Liberan a familiares de Zhenli Ye Gon," *Milenio diario*, June 5, 2012.

35. The available information on the case of General Mario Acosta Chaparro can be found at: https://wikileaks.org/wiki/Bank _Julius_Baer_millions_of_USD_in_trust_for_Mexican_mass _murderer_and_drug_trafficker_Arturo_Acosta_Chapparo,_1998.

36. Cf. Pascal Gauchon and Jean-Marc Huissoud (coords.), *Las 100 palabras de la geopolítica*, Madrid, Akal, 2013, 125 pp. Hans Kelsen, *Derecho y lógica*, Mexico, Coyoacán, 2012, p. 8, note 1.

37. Jacobo G. García, "El fantasma del paramilitarismo en México," *El Mundo*, September 27, 2011: http://www.elmundo.es /america/2011/09/28/mexico/1317161989.html.

38. Cf. Mission of the International Commission of Jurists (ICJ), *Socavando el Estado de derecho y consolidando la impunidad*, Colombia, ICJ, 2005, 79 pp.

39. CNN, "EU tuvo reportes de que empresarios contrataron paramilitares en Juárez," March 17, 2011: http://expansion.mx /nacional/2011/03/17/eu-tuvo-reportes-de-que-empresarios -contrataron-paramilitares-en-juarez.

40. Campo Algonodero ruling (IACHR), Santiago de Chile, 2009, 167 pp.: http://www.corteidh.or.cr/docs/casos/articulos/seriec _205_esp.pdf.

41. Barrón Cruz has described the situation as follows: "What can be seen in our country as a result of the 'war on drug trafficking' is the consolidation of a *penal state* based on intolerance, as well as in the 'war on poverty,' due to the necessity of gaining the support of the comfortable classes and those terrorized by insecurity. This has led to the institution of a highly repressive penal policy based

around the 'culture of emergency and criminal exceptionality,' which includes, among many other measures, new types of highly punitive punishments, cuts to prison programs aimed at certain types of inmates and a greater military and police presence." Cf. Martín Gabriel Barrón Cruz, *Violencia y seguridad en México en el umbral del siglo XXI*, Mexico, Instituto Nacional de Ciencias Penales, 2012, p. 187.

42. Agamben explains that "this transformation of a provisional and exceptional measure into a technique of government threatens radically to alter—in fact, has already palpably altered—the structure and meaning of the traditional distinction between constitutional forms." See Giorgio Agamben, *State of Exception*, Chicago, University of Chicago Press, 2005, p. 2.

43. "El estado no ha cumplido su función de proteger a la gente," *Excélsior*, October 14, 2011: http://www.excelsior.com.mx/index .php?m=nota&id_nota=774833.

44. For example, the 2008 penal reform: cf. Raúl Carrancá y Rivas, *Reforma constitucional de 2008 en materia de justicia penal y seguridad pública. Variaciones críticas*, Mexico, Porrúa, 2010, 126 pp.

45. Liliana Alcántara, "La ONU regaña a México por derechos humanos," *El Universal*, October 13, 2009: http://www.eluniversal .com.mx/notas/632860.html.

46. "Critica Kofi Annan estrategia anti-narco de Calderón," Animal Político, October 19, 2012. Annan stated: "He's got lots of people killed": http://www.animalpolitico.com/2012/10 /estrategia-antidrogas-de-calderon-no-ha-funcionado-ha-muerto -mucha-gente-kofi-annan/.

47. Cf. http://www.dof.gob.mx/nota_detalle.php?codigo=5310763 &fecha=16/08/2013; also "Piden en EU combatir narco como terrorismo," *Reforma*, December 16, 2010.

48. Pedro Diego Tzuc, "Capturan a presunto miembro de Hezbolá," *Reforma*, September 9, 2012.

49. "La mano de obra nacional es más barata que la china," *El Informador*, October 23, 2012: http://www.informador.com.mx/

economia/2009/104929/6/la-mano-de-obra-nacional-es-mas
-barata-que-la-china.htm.

2. Years of Lead

1. On January 22, 2007, weeks after his inauguration, President
Felipe Calderón Hinojosa promised to win "the war" on organized
crime during a public meeting of the National Public Security
Council. Since that meeting, his anti-drug trafficking operations,
which constituted the most important policy of his administration, have been known as the "war on drug trafficking": this is how
both he and the members of his cabinet have repeatedly referred
to these operations. Cf: http://www.jornada.unam.mx/2007
/01/23/index.php?section=politica&article=003n1pol. According
to Article 89, Section VIII of the Mexican Constitution, the powers
and duties of the president include "declaring war in the name of
the United Mexican States, pursuant to a previous law of the
Congress of the Union." The Calderón administration therefore
violated constitutional principles in declaring his "war" on drug
trafficking.

2. The official reports of the U.S. government, as well as those of
Stratfor, which specializes in matters of global security, have a good
reputation as sources of information. Cf. Ana Langner, "Stratfor:
Mexico, adicto a las narcoganancias," *El Economista*, August 22, 2012.

3. Ulrich Beck, *Poder y contrapoder en la era global*, Barcelona,
Paidós, 2004, p. 38.

4. Nallely Ortigoza, "Compran chinos Ciudad Juárez," *Reforma*,
March 30, 2012.

5. In the case of Zeta leader Heriberto Lazcano, the official story
states that he was killed in combat and that his corpse was stolen,
cf. Jorge Carrasco Arraizaga and Juan Alberto Zedillo, "La caída y
la sucesión," *Proceso*, October 14, 2012; Patricia Dávila, "El
cadáver exhibido no es de Lazca," *Proceso*, October 14, 2012. In
federal intelligence circles, a story circulated in which Lazcano cut
a deal with a U.S. government agency and turned himself in; his
death was faked.

6. Peña Nieto promised "planning, prevention, human rights protections, institutional coordination and transformation": cf. http://www.enriquepenanieto.com/compromisos-nacionales/com -promiso/recuperar-la-paz-y-la-libertad; the speech given by the president on December 17, 2012 at the Second Extraordinary Session of the National Public Security Council: https://www.gob. mx/presidencia/en/videos/sesion-extraordinaria-consejo-nacional -de-seguridad-publica-mexico; J. J. Esquivel, "En sigilo, crea el gobierno el Centro Nacional de Inteligencia," *Proceso*, January 13, 2013, pp. 6–9. The goal of this center is to head off the penetration of the Binational Intelligence Office, which is operated by U.S. intelligence agencies.

7. Jorge Carrasco Araizaga, "Por la SEDENA se vale todo," *Proceso*, July 22, 2012.

8. "Propone Senado de EU dar mil mdd a México para depurar policías," *Milenio*, July 12, 2012.

9. Juan Veledíaz, "Una historia de amor y espionaje," *Proceso*, February 21, 2010.

10. Chris Arsenault, "Mexican Official: CIA "manages" drug trade," *Al Jazeera*, July 24,2012: http://www.aljazeera.com/ indepth /features/2012/07/2012721152715628181.html.

11. For example, Ignacio Coronel, Javier García Morales, Vicente Mayo Zambada, José Luis Esparragoza and Mario Acosta Chaparro.

12. Wiezman explains: "These days, military manuals tend to employ concepts such as *simultaneity, networks, overlap, symmetry* and *disequilibrium*, describing a Hobbesian nightmare of chaotic connections: a periodic 'global civil war' of all against all." Cf. Eyal Weizman, *A través de los muros*, Madrid, Errata Naturae, 2012, p. 31.

13. Juan David Pastrana Berdejo and Esbert Benavente Chorro, "La reforma en México," in *Implementación del proceso acusatorio de oralidad en Latinoamérica*, Mexico, Flores Editor y Distribuidor / Facultad de Derecho UAEM, 2010, pp. 219–298.

14. Gustavo Castillo García, "Trabajan para agencias estadounidenses," *La Jornada*, December 18, 2011.

15. NOTIMEX, "América Latina es nuestro 'patio trasero': secretario de Estado de EU, John Kerry," April 17, 2013. A study of the history of this posture can be found in Grace Livingstone, *America's Backyard: The United States and Latin America from the Monroe Doctrine to the War on Terror*, London, Zed Books, 2009, 256 pp. "Lista base militar: espiará el Pentagano a México desde Puebla," *Vanguardia*, December 22, 2011: http://www.vanguardia.com.mx/listabase militarespiaraelpentagonoamexicodesdepuebla-1177527.html

16. "Hubo más de 7.000 asesinatos en seis meses," *El Economista / AFP*, August 9, 2012. Both the National Citizen Observatory for Security, Justice and Legality and Lantia have questioned the official figures. According to the non-governmental organization México Evalúa, there were 101,000 homicides between 2006 and 2012, a figure that approximates the casualties from the wars in Iraq and the former Yugoslavia: Rolando Herrera, "Estiman 101 mil asesinados en sexenio," *Reforma*, November 27, 2012. Robert Sandels, "Militarization and Political Crisis in Mexico," Global Research, USA, September 4, 2013: http://www.globalresearch.ca /militarization-and-political-crisis-in-mexico/5347998.

17. See the position of Justice José Ramón Cossío Díaz, who argues that, according to the Mexican Constitution, the army may only carry out peacetime operations that have a strict connection to military discipline and in spaces that are assigned to it (bases, barracks, headquarters, etc.). Policing duties carried out by the army are unconstitutional: http://es.scribd.com/doc/102349639/Cossio-001. For a partial interpretation of this issue by the Legal Advisor to the Federal Executive, see Miguel Alessio Robles, "Réplica/Niega Ejecutivo violar la Constitución," *Reforma*, letters page, August 10, 2012.

18. Jorge Carrasco Araizaga and J. J. Esquivel, "Atrapar al Chapo," *Proceso*, August 12, 2012.

19. Gustavo Castillo García, "Federales dispararon 152 veces contra los agentes de la CIA en Tres Marías," *La Jornada*, September 15, 2012.

20. Alfredo Méndez, "Levantan el primer arraigo en la gestión del procurador Jesús Murillo Karam," *La Jornada*, December 17, 2012: http://www.jornada.unam.mx/2012/12/17/politica/013n1pol.

21. For example, it has been reported that General Acosta Chaparro was assassinated because, in collaboration with the CIA, he was investigating General Enrique Cervantes Aguirre, who had once jailed him. According to this version, Cervantes Aguirre is implicated in the corruption of the Mexican Army by drug traffickers and is on the radar of U.S. intelligence agencies: cf. Isabel Arvide, *Mis generales*, Mexico, Planeta, 2012, p. 301. Cervantes Aguirre is one of Mexico's most powerful generals: he has a special intelligence team at his service and his former subordinates are among the army's most influential officers.

22. This cable, which was released by WikiLeaks, was signed by Secretary of State Condoleeza Rice, cf. Anabel Hernández, "Pactan en secreto la Marina y EU," Reforma, August 29, 2012.

23. On the significance of the term "smooth" in ultracontemporary military thinking, cf. Eyal Weizman, *A través de las puertas*, op. cit. p. 57.

24. On the importance of information networks to the contemporary field of battle, cf. John Arquilla and David Ronfeldt, *Networks and Netwars: The Future of Terror, Crime and Militancy*, op. cit., 2001, 352 pp.

25. To examine the American ideology of integration as the establishment of a common "security" space that absorbs Mexico's infrastructure, borders, armed forces, airspace, intelligence, strategic resources and opportunities for economic development, cf. Pedro Aspe, et. al. "Building a North American Community: Report of an Independent Task Force," US, Canada, Mexico, Council on Foreign Relations/Canadian Council of Chief Executives/Consejo Mexicano de Asuntos Internacionales, 2005, 47 pp. For a critical analysis from a legal perspective of this integration and Mexico's asymmetrical role in it, cf. Amada María Arley Orduña, *Más allá del TLCAN. ASPAN ¿qué es y a dónde vamos?*, Mexico, Porrúa, 2001.

26. Report: *San Pedro Sula (Honduras), la ciudad más violenta del mundo; Juárez, la segunda*, Mexico, Consejo Ciudadano para la Seguridad Pública y Justicia Penal, A.C., 2012, 63 pp.

27. The data and analysis in this section are taken from Javier Hernández, "Lucha contra el narcotráfico en zonas urbanas:

Monterrey," United Nations Office on Drugs and Crime, September 2012, 34 pp.: https://www.slideshare.net/Gobernabilidad/unodc sep2012-jh1.

28. The criminal cartography of Monterrey and the criminal practices described here are taken from the Southern Pulse report, "Monterrey Street Gangs," Latin America, Southern Pulse, March 2012, 23 pp.

29. Southern Pulse, "Monterrey Street Gangs," Latin America, Southern Pulse, March 2012, p. 8.

30. The criminal cartography of Acapulco and the criminal practices described here are taken from the Southern Pulse report, "Acapulco Criminal Environment," Latin America, Southern Pulse, June 2012, 23 pp.

31. Luis Kuryaki, "Revela Wikileaks a Ciudad Juárez como 'proyecto piloto' en guerra vs. narco," Juarezland, December 2, 2010: http://juarezland.wordpress.com/2010/12/02/revela-wiki leaks-a-ciudad-juarez-como-proyecto-piloto-en-guerra-vs-narco/; Secretaría de la Defensa Nacional, *Tercer Informe de Labores*, Mexico, SEDENA, 162 pp.: http://www.sedena.gob.mx/pdf/informes /3er_informe_de_labores.pdf.

32. Amnesty International Report 2010, London, AI, pp. 223–226: https://www.amnesty.org/en/documents/pol10/001/2010/en/.

33. The criminal cartography of Ciudad Juárez and the criminal practices described here are taken from the Southern Pulse report, "Ciudad Juárez Criminal Environment," Latin America, Southern Pulse, October 2012, 47 pp.

34. The criminal cartography of Guadalajara and the criminal practices described here are taken from the Southern Pulse report, "Guadalajara Criminal Environment," Latin America, Southern Pulse, August 2012, 19 pp.

35. At the beginning of 2013, the Mexico City government launched "Plan Central Shield" with Mexico State, Morelos and Hidalgo in order to jointly confront challenges on issues of security, water, transportation and the environment: "Mancera arranca hoy el Plan Escudo Centro," *La Razón*, February 2, 2013.

36. Jésica Zermeño, "Parte de guerra," *Enfoque* supplement, *Reforma*, September 16, 2013, pp. 7–9; Annual Report, SIPRI, June 2010: http://www.sipri.org.

37. Stephen Graham, *Cities Under Siege: The New Military Urbanism*, New York/London, Verso, 2011, 432 pp.

38. Allan Feldman, "Securocratic Wars of Public Safety," in *Interventions: International Journal of Postcolonial Studies*, London/New York, vol. 6, no. 3, 2004, pp. 330–250.

39. María Crespo, "Las cámaras de seguridad se multiplican por todo el mundo," *El Mundo*, August 4, 2010: http://www.elmundo .es/elmundo/2010/08/04/internacional/1280938576.html; in recent years, the Mexico City government has installed close to 15,000 cameras and it plans on installing another 7,000 more: "Alcalde Mancera quiere más cámaras de seguridad para Ciudad de México," Mexico, *Ventas de Seguridad*, December 10, 2012: http://www.ventasdeguridad.com/201212106784/noticias/emp resas/alcalde-mancera-quiere-mas-camaras-de-seguridad-para -ciudad-de-mexico.html.

40. Stephen Graham, *Cities Under Siege*, op. cit.

41. Francisco Tucho Fernández, "La manipulación de la informa-ción en los conflictos armados: tácticas y estrategias," Spain, 17 pp.: http://www2.uned.es/ntedu/espanol/master/segundo/modulos /comunicacion%20audiovisual/tucho2.pdf.

3. Anamorphosis of the Victim

1. José Zamora Grant, *Derecho victimal. La víctima en el nuevo sis-tema penal mexicano*, Mexico, Instituto Nacional de Ciencias Penales, 2009, 215 pp.

2. Alejandro Linares Zárate, *La Justicia. Su simbología y valores que concurren en su aplicación*, Mexico, UAMEX, 2005, 10 pp.: http://web.uaemex.mx/identidad/docs/JUSTICIA.pdf; on the pyra-midal structure of positive law, in which each norm is based on a norm of a higher order, cf., Hans Kelsen, *Teoría pura del derecho*, Mexico, Éxodo, 2006, 174 pp.

3. Franz Kafka, *The Trial: Definitive Edition*, New York, The Modern Library, 1956.

4. Baltrušaitis writes that "anamorphosis—a word that appears in the 17th century, though related to previous compositions—proceeds via an inversion of elements and functions. Rather than a gradual reduction to their visible boundaries, it is a dilation, a projection of forms outside themselves, executed in such a way that they are configured towards a specific point of view: destruction via re-assembly, escape implying a return […] An anamorphosis is a puzzle, a monster, a prodigy," cf.: Jurgis Baltrušaitis, *Les perspectives dépravées. Tome 2, Anamorphoses*, Paris, Flamarion, 1996, pp. 7–8.

5. The argument here follows the line of Agamben: "bare life, that is, the life of *homo sacer* (sacred man), who *may be killed and yet not sacrificed* […]. An obscure figure of archaic Roman law, in which human life is included in the juridical order (*ordinamento*) solely in the form of its exclusion (that is, of its capacity to be killed)," cf., Giorgio Agamben, *Homo Sacer: Sovereign Power and Bare Life*, Stanford, Stanford University Press, 1998, p. 8. "Its capacity to be killed" is a fact in Mexican society, where the impunity rate for violent crime is absolute.

6. "Homicidas de edecán, al servicio de El Teo," *El Universal*, August 8, 2009. Also: http://blogs.periodistadigital.com/hermosillo.php/2009/08/07/p245576.

7. Case recorded by the author, the victim's name has been changed to protect their identity.

8. Case recorded by the author, the victim's name has been changed to protect their identity.

9. Case recorded by the author, the victim's name has been changed to protect their identity.

10. Human Rights Watch, *Ni Seguridad, Ni Derechos. Ejecuciones, desapariciones y tortura en la "guerra contra el narcotráfico" de México*, New York, 2011, p. 72.

11. Ibid, p. 68.

12. Case recorded by the author, the victim's name has been changed to protect their identity.

13. John Gibler, *To Die in Mexico*, San Francisco, City Lights Books, 2011, pp. 7–13.

14. "Patrulla fronteriza mata a un mexicano," *El Universal/La Vanguardia*, October 11, 2012: http://www.vanguardia.com.mx /desdeeupatrullafronterizamataajovenmexicano-1392731.html.

15. U.S. Navy, *Survival, Evasion, Resistance and Escape Handbook*, U.S.A., Department of Defense, 2011.

16. Article 3 of the Geneva Convention of 1949, which deals with the treatment of prisoners of war, prohibits "the passing of sentences and the carrying out of executions without previous judgment pronounced by a regularly constituted court, affording all the judicial guarantees which are recognized as indispensable by civilized peoples": https://ihl-databases.icrc.org/applic/ihl/ihl.nsf /Article.xsp?action=openDocument&documentId=BAA341028 EBFF1E8C12563CD00519E66.

17. A critical analysis of the origin and meaning of this phrase, as well as its current uses, can be found in Jimmy Sun, *Inter Arma Silent Leges*, U.S.A., CS 199r Final Project, May 14, 2006.

18. Barry W. Watts, *Clausewitzian Friction and Future War*, Washington, McNair Paper 68, October 1996 (Revised August 2004), p. 1 and following: https://www.clausewitz.com/readings /Watts-Friction3.pdf.

19. Nicolas Skrotzky, *La Terre victime de guerres*, Sang de la Terre, Paris, 2002, 319 pp.

20. Slavoj Žižek, *Looking Awry: An Introduction to Jacques Lacan through Popular Culture*, Cambridge (MA), MIT Press, 1992, 188 pp.

21. Jurgis Baltrušaitis, *Les perspectives dépravées*, op. cit., pp. 125–160; Slavoj Žižek, *Looking Awry*, op. cit., pp. 30–55.

22. For a study of the generations of warfare, and in particular the fourth generation, see Thomas Hammes, *The Sling and the Stone*, Saint Paul (Minnesota), Zenith Press, 2006, 366 pp.

23. Eyal Weizman, *A través de las puertas*, op. cit. p. 22. Also, Sean J. A. Edwards, *Swarming on the Battlefield: Past, Present and Future*, Santa Monica (California), Rand, 2000, 108 pp.

24. On the effects of social media on drug trafficking in Mexico, Andrés Monroy-Hernández, Emre Kiciman, Danah Boyd and Scott Counts, "Narcotweets: Social Media in Wartime," U.S.A., Microsoft Research, 2011, pp. 515–518: https://www.microsoft.com/en-us /research/wp-content/uploads/2016/02/ICWSM12-093.pdf.

25. Eyal Weizman, *A través de las puertas*, op. cit., pp. 10–11.

26. Rubén Martín, "Narco y violencia en Guadalajara," *El Economista*, March 12, 2012: http://eleconomista.com.mx/columnas /columna-especial-politica/2012/03/12/narco-violencia-guadalajara.

27. René Ramón and Israel Dávila, "Paralizan rumores sobre violencia el oriente del Edomex," *La Jornada*, September 7, 2012: http://www.jornada.unam.mx/2012/09/07/estados/032n1est.

28. "Desmantelan una red de comunicación de Los Zetas," *Excélsior*, August 24, 2012: http://www.excelsior.com.mx/2012/08/24 /nacional/855319.

29. Jean Clair, *Hubris. La fabrique du monstre dans l'art moderne*, Paris, Gallimard, 2012, 189 pp.

30. For an example of the official propaganda of the war on drug trafficking, Alejandro Poiré Romero, *¿Por qué el narcotráfico se hizo más violento en los últimos años?*, Mexico, Gobierno Federal, August 21, 2011: http://calderon.presidencia.gob.mx/blog/alejandro-poire -romero/; also: https://www.youtube.com/watch?v=rPFR0imY1f4.

31. The description of these vehicles is taken from "Blindados del narco, monstruos inoperantes," *La Razón*, June 18, 2011.

32. Jameson argues that machines as icons "are still visible emblems, sculptural nodes of energy which give tangibility and figuration to the motive energies," Frederic Jameson, *Postmodernism, or the Cultural Logic of Late Capitalism*, New York, Verso, 1991, p. 36; Deena Weinstein, *Heavy Metal: The Music and Its Culture*, New York, Da Capo Press, 2000, 368 pp.

4. Global War on Drug Trafficking

1. Reuters, "El consumo de drogas en Estados Unidos alcanza su máximo histórico," *Expansión*, September 17, 2010: http://expansion.mx/mundo/2010/09/17/el-consumo-de-drogas-estados-unidos-alcanza-su-maximo-historico; UNODC, *World Drug Report 2012*, New York, 2012, p. 18.

2. OCTA 2009, *EU Organized Crime Threat Assessment*, EUROPOL, 2009, 63 pp.: https://www.europol.europa.eu/sites/default/files/documents/octa2009_0.pdf.

3. Homero Campa, "Los Zetas y Ndrangheta: la conexión," *Proceso*, November 15, 2009: pp. 51–55. Also, Cynthia Rodríguez, *Contacto en Italia*, Mexico, Debate, 267 pp.

4. UNODC, *The Threat of Narco-Trafficking in the Americas*, United Nations Office on Drugs and Crime, October 2008, pp. 31 and following.

5. Moisés Naím, *Illicit: How Smugglers, Traffickers and Copycats are Hijacking the Global Economy*, New York, Anchor, 2006, 352 pp.; Francesco Forgione, *Mafia Export: Cómo la 'Ndrangheta, la Cosa Nostra y la Camorra han colonizado el mundo*, Barcelona, Anagrama, 2009, 386 pp.

6. Criticism of policies that prohibit drugs and criminalize users can be seen in *War on Drugs: Report of the Global Commission on Drug Policy*, June 2011, http://www.globalcommissionondrugs.org/reports/the-war-on-drugs/. Also, Araceli Manjón-Cabeza, *La solución. La legalización de las drogas*, Mexico, Debate, 2012, 318 pp.

A criticism of drug legalization can be found in Mark Kleiman, *Contención del crimen organizado y no organizado*, Mexico, INACIPE, 2011, 29 pp. To understand the hemispheric drug strategy, which recommends "optimizing" control over the supply and demand of drugs, see: http://www.cicad.oas.org/Main/Template.asp?File=/main/aboutcicad/basicdocuments/strategy_2010_eng.asp.

7. There were 493 decapitations in 2011 alone, "Decapitaciones se desatan en este sexenio," October 28, 2012: http://archivo.eluniversal.com.mx/notas/879375.html. According to federal prosecutors,

there were 2,611 decapitations between 2007 and 2011: "La anulación del crimen organizado," *Milenio diario*, November 12, 2012.

8. Report of the Press Emblem Campaign, PEC, October 2, 2012, Geneva: http://www.pressemblem.ch/10399.html.

9. "71 por ciento del territorio nacional bajo control del narco," *Proceso/Apro*, September 1, 2010.

10. Stratfor Global Intelligence, *Mexico in Crisis: Lost Borders and the Struggle for Regional Status*, Austin (TX), Stratfor Books, 2009, 270 pp.

11. See above, chapter 1, note 8.

12. Anabel Hernández, *Narcoland: The Mexican Drug Lords and Their Godfathers*, New York, Verso, 2013, 384 pp.

13. UNODC, 2010 Report, New York, April 2010, 71 pp.: https://www.unodc.org/documents/wdr/WDR_2010/World_Drug _Report_2010_lo-res.pdf. Also, European Police Office, Europol SOCTA 2013, European Union, 2013, 52 pp.; In 2013, the Organization of American States issued an analytical report titled *The Drug Problem in the Americas*, Washington, OAS/Secretary General, 2013, 114 pp. Among other points, it suggests that governments consider decriminalizing drug consumption and legalizing marijuana.

14. Cf. Froylán Enciso, "Los fracasos del chantaje. Régimen de prohibición de drogas y narcotráfico," in Arturo Alvarado and Mónica Serrano (coords.), vol. 15, Mexico, COLMEX, 2010, pp. 61–104.

15. Zygmunt Bauman, *Liquid Times: Living in an Age of Uncertainty*, Cambridge (UK), Polity Press, 2007, 128 pp.

16. NOTIMEX, "EU mantiene control efectivo en 15 por ciento de la frontera," *El Universal*, February 15, 2011.

17. Patrick Picouet and Jean-Pierre Renard, *Les frontières mondiales: Origenes et dynamiques*, Nantes, Éditions du temps, 2007, 159 pp.

18. Katy Connolly, "US border violence: Myth or reality?" BBC/El Paso, Texas, July 28, 2010: http://www.bbc.com/news/world-us -canada-10779151.

19. José Luna, "Circulan casi 15 millones de armas ilegales en México," *El Sol de México*, February 24, 2008. In 2014, according to the investigator Magda Coss Noguera, there were over 20 million uncontrolled firearms in Mexico.

20. José Díaz Briseño, "Pega a ATF escándalo por tráfico de armas," *Reforma*, March 5, 2011.

21. Jorge Fernández Menéndez, *Narcotráfico y poder*, Mexico, Rayuela, 1999, 235 pp. This network of complicity was implicated in two contemporary assassinations that have been attributed to the fact that the victims had discovered the connections between drug traffickers and the Mexican and U.S. governments, which had then been kept confidential: the first was the Mexican journalist Manuel Buendía, killed in 1984, and the second was the American DEA agent Enrique Camarena, killed one year later (Jorge Fernández Menéndez, *Narcotráfico y poder*, op. cit., p. 24). This two-headed ghost accompanied the degradation of Mexico and the ambiguity of the United States with regard to the drug problem at the continental level, as well as its relations with the countries to its south. According to the DEA agents who were operating in Mexico at the time, the CIA carried out both assassinations: J. Jesús Esquivel, "La historia secreta detrás del asesinato de Camarena," *Proceso*, October 19, 2013: http://www.proceso.com.mx/355922/la-historia -secreta-detras-del-asesinato-de-camarena.

22. The Central American Free Trade Agreement (CAFTA), the Central American Citizen Safety Partnership (CACSP) and the Central American Regional Security Initiative (CARSI).

23. Mike Whitney, "Is the CIA behind Mexico's Bloody Drug War?" Global Research, April 26, 2010: https://www.global research.ca/is-the-cia-behind-mexico-s-bloody-drug-war/18877.

24. The ultracontemporary military thinking of the United States can be seen in the Joint Vision 2010 document, U.S., Department of Defense, 1996, 39 pp.: http://webapp1.dlib.indiana.edu/virtual _disk_library/index.cgi/4240529/FID378/pdfdocs/2010/Jv2010.pdf.

25. Blanche Petrich, "Intentó EU incluir en plan Mérida un acuerdo antiterrorista," *La Jornada*, February 12, 2011.

26. J. Jaime Hernández, "EU teme liga de Zetas y Al Qaeda," *El Universal*, February 10, 2011: http://archivo.eluniversal.com.mx /notas/743834.html; Cynthia Rodríguez, *Contacto en Italia*, Mexico, Debate, 2009, 267 pp.

27. J. Jaime Hernández, "Frontera sur de México, un serio problema: EU," *El Universal*, April 6, 2011: http://archivo.eluniversal.com.m /nacion/184579.html.

28. Peter Dale Scott, *American War Machine: Deep Politics, the CIA Global Drug Connection and the Road to Afghanistan*, Lanham (Maryland), Rowman & Littlefield Publishers, 2010, 408 pp.

29. See the report: Open Society Foundations, Globalizing Torture: CIA Secret Rendition and Extraordinary Rendition, USA, Open Society Justice Initiative, 2013, 212 pp., retrieved on February 8, 2013 from https://www.opensocietyfoundations.org /reports/globalizing-torture-cia-secret-detention-and-extraordinary -rendition. As has been argued by Tim Weiner, author of the officialist history of the CIA titled *Legacy of Ashes* (USA, Anchor, 2007, 848 pp.), the agency "is no longer an espionage institution and has instead become a paramilitary organization dedicated to, among other operations, the selective assassination of its enemies" (Anna Grau, "La CIA se dedica al asesinato selectivo," *ABC*, March 8, 2010). In terms of the agency's extrajudicial operations, particularly its "selective assassinations" through on-the-ground operations or drone attacks, see Mark Mazzetti, *The Way of the Knife: The CIA, a Secret Army, and a War at the Ends of the Earth*, New York, Penguin, 2013, 381 pp.

30. Jorge Carrasco A. and J.J. Esquivel, "El gran espía," *Proceso*, November 14, 2010, pp. 6–9.

31. Office on Drugs and Crime, *The Threat of Narco-Trafficking in the Americas*, New York, UN, 2008, p. 3 and following.

32. UNODC, *World Drugs Report*: New York, 2010, 100 pp.

33. Medea Benjamin, *Killing by Remote Control*, New York/ London, OR Books, 2012, 262 pp.; Elizabeth Bumiller (NYT), "Matar a distancia," *El País*, July 31, 2012; Doris Gómora, "Nuevos 'guardias' de EU en frontera con México," *El Universal*, May 4,

2012: http://archivo.eluniversal.com.mx/notas/845035.html. Pepe Flores, "La Marina de México produce su primer vehículo aéreo no tripulado," alt1040.com, August 16, 2012: https://hipertextual.com /2012/08/marina-drones.

34. President Felipe Calderón allowed U.S. drones to carry out espionage activities in Mexican airspace. This was the typical executive order that violates constitutional principles: Dana Priest, "U.S. role at a crossroads in Mexico's intelligence war on the cartels," *The Washington Post*, April 27, 2013. For a defense of privacy, Jay Stanley and Catherine Crump, *Protecting Privacy from Aerial Surveillance: Recommendations for Government Use of Drone Aircraft*, New York, American Civil Liberties Union, December 2011, 16 pp. "Muerte con drones, similar a ejecución extrajudicial: AI," May 22, 2013: http://www.eluniversal.com.mx/notas/ 924732.html.

Epilogue: Planetary Transhumanism

1. On the origin of the term, Julian Huxley, "Transhumanism," *New Bottles of New Wine*, Chatto & Windus, 1957, pp. 13–17: http://www.transhumanism.org/index.php/WTA/more/huxley/; for a contemporary position on the topic: Ray Kurzweil, *The Singularity Is Near: When Humans Transcend Biology*, New York, Penguin, 2006, 672 pp. Half a century ago, the philosopher Günther Anders described a threat that has now been realized: "The triumph of the world of devices consists of the elimination of the distinction between technical and social structures, which have been left without an object. The proper functioning of macrodevices is the precondition of the functioning of microdevices, which, seen from the perspective of the macrodevices, are reduced to mere pieces of a larger device. Likewise, each macrodevice, to the extent that it wishes to function and function well, must coordinate itself with other devices, including other macrodevices. As fantastic as it may seem, this demonstrates that devices have as their fundamental goal a situation in which there is only a single comprehensive device, or rather, The Device: that device that 'incorporates and synthesizes' all devices and that makes everything work. This is a key concept, as the contemporary world of devices can only be understood *ex futuro*, through its latent final idea: devices = the world." See Günther Anders, *La obsolescencia del hombre*,

vol. II, Valencia, Pre-Textos, 2011, p. 115. Agamben argues that it would not be misguided to define the extreme phase of capitalist development we are currently living through as one of the mass accumulation and proliferation of devices, and even though there have been devices ever since the dawn of *homo sapiens*, today there is not a single instant in which the lives of individuals are not being modeled, contaminated or controlled by a device of some sort: Giorgio Agamben, *Che cos'è un dispositivo?*, Rome, Nottetempo, 2006, 35 pp.

2. On the U.S. Department of Defense's Unified Combatant Commands, which are distributed in every region of the world: https://en.wikipedia.org/wiki/Unified_combatant_command.

3. Francis Fukuyama, *America at the Crossroads: Democracy, Power and the Neoconservative Legacy*, New Haven (CT), Yale University Press, 2007, 264 pp.; Kishore Mahbubani, *The Great Convergence: Asia, the West, and the Logic of One World*, New York, PublicAffairs, 2013, 328 pp.; Nathan Gardels, "La lógica de un solo mundo," *El País*, January 17, 2013.

4. Bruno Latour, *Re-ensamblar lo social. Una introducción a la teoría del actor-red*. Buenos Aires, Manantiel, 2008, p. 260.

5. Ulrich Beck, *Poder y contrapoder en la era global*, op. cit. p. 71.

6. Anthony Romano, *Joint Vision 2010: Developing the System of Systems*, U.S.A., Air Command and Staff College, Maxwell Air Force, 1998, 43 pp.

7. On the military origin of the Internet: Ronda Hauben, "From ARPANET to the Internet," New York, Columbia University, 1998: http://www.columbia.edu/~rh120/other/tcpdigest_paper.txt; on the ECHELON interception system: *European Parliament, Report on the existence of a global system for the interception of private and commercial communications (ECHELON interception system) (2001/ 2098(INI)), 2001*, 204 pp.; a detailed analysis of the civilian and military uses of control and surveillance can be found in Thomas Allmer, *Towards a Critical Theory of Informational Capitalism*, Frankfurt am Main, Peter Land, Europaischer Verlag der Wissenschaften, 2012, 136 pp. On the U.S. National Security Agency's PRISM program: Glenn Greenwald and Ewen MacAskill,

"NSA Prism program taps in to user data of Apple, Google and others," *The Guardian*, June 7, 2013: https://www.theguardian.com/world/2013/jun/06/us-tech-giants-nsa-data. A criticism of global espionage can be found in Ulrich Beck, "El riesgo para la libertad," *El País*, August 30, 2013, p. 21.

8. National Intelligence Council, *Global Trends 2030: Alternative Worlds*. U.S.A., NIC, 2012, 40 pp.

9. Joint Vision 2020, *America's Military-Preparing for Tomorrow*, U.S.A., Department of Defense, 2000, 40 pp.

10. Ibid, p. 4.

11. P.W. Singer, *Corporate Warriors: The Rise of the Privatized Military Industry*, Ithica (NY), Cornell University Press, 2007, 260 pp.

12. Ibid, p. 8.

13. *HBR's 10 Must Reads on Strategy (including featured article "What Is Strategy?" by Michael E. Porter)*, U.S.A., Harvard Business Review, 2011, 288 pp.

14. Ibid, p. 20.

15. Allmer synthesizes the approach that observes a neutrality in control and surveillance technology: "Non-panoptic notions of Internet surveillance either use a neutral concept that assumes there are enabling effects such as protection and security as well as constraining effects such as control or a positive concept that identifies comical, playful, amusing, and even enjoyable characteristics of surveillance where everyone has the opportunity to surveil. In addition, these approaches tend to reject the proposition that surveillance mechanisms are dominated by political and economic actors and see monitoring not necessarily as annoying and disturbing. In non-panoptic notions of the Internet, surveillance is understood as a useful and effective management tool and as fair methods and procedures of monitoring individuals online." Thomas Allmer, *Towards a Critical Theory of Surveillance in Informational Capitalism*, op. cit. p. 81.

16. The characteristics of the new model of control and surveillance are described in Gary T. Marx, "What's new about the 'New Surveillance'? Classifying for Change and Continuity," *Surveillance and Society*, 1 (1), Surveillance Studies Network, 2002 pp. 9–29: https://ojs.library.queensu.ca/index.php/surveillance-and-society/article/view/3391/3354.

17. A detailed discussion of this issue can be found in Gary T. Marx, "An Ethics for the New Surveillance," *The Information Society*, no. 14, 1998, pp. 171–185.

18. Stephen Graham, *Cities Under Siege*, op. cit.

19. Ibid; Harvey Molotch, *Against Security: How We Go Wrong at Airports, Subways, and Other Sites of Ambiguous Danger*, Princeton, Princeton University Press, 2012, 278 pp.; Anna Minton, *Ground Control: Fear and Happiness in the Twenty-First-Century City*, London, Penguin, 2012, 288 pp.

20. On the "law of the enemy": Günther Jakobs, *El pensamiento filosófico y jurídico de Günther Jakobs*, Mexico, Flores Editor y Distribuidor. A criticism of the application of this theory in Mexico can be seen in: Miguel Ángel Mancera, "El Derecho penal del enemigo en México," *Revista Penal*, Mexico, pp. 141–160.

21. Stephen Graham, *Cities Under Siege*, op. cit. See also the futurist vision of the organization Great Transition: http://www.gtinitiative.org.

22. For cultural interventions on the issue of control and surveillance: Ana García Angulo, *Intervenciones en el arte contemporaneo: CCTV*, Facultad de Bellas Artes de Madrid, Departamento de Pintura, 2007, 79 pp.

23. Paul Raskin, Tariq Banuri, Gilberto Gallopín, Pablo Gutman, Al Hammond, Robert Kates and Rob Swart, *La gran transición: la promesa y la attración del futuro*, Santiago de Chile, UN/ECLAC/Stockholm Environment Institute/Global Scenario Group, 2006, 79 pp.

24. Felipe González Márquez, et al., *Project Europe 2030: Challenges and Opportunities. A Report to the European Council by the Reflection*

Group on the Future of the EU 2030, European Union, May 2010, p.12.

25. Ibid, p. 33.

26. Ibid, p. 35.

27. Ibid, p. 36.

28. Pilar del Castillo Vera, *Report on a new Digital Agenda for Europe: 2015*, European Parliament, Committee on Research, Industry and Energy, 2010.

29. TNS, Presentación del estudio Mobile Life, Spain, 2012, pp. 27 and 28: https://www.slideshare.net/TNSspain/presentacin-del -estudio-mobile-life.

30. Thomas Allmer, *Towards a Critical Theory of Surveillance in Informational Capitalism*, op. cit.

31. The U.S. Information Awareness Office was established in 2002 by the Defense Advanced Research Projects Agency (DARPA) in order to achieve Total Information Awareness (TIA). In 2003, when its funding was taken away by Congress, the program continued to operate under different names, continuing this totalizing project. Cf. Elliot D. Cohen, *Mass Surveillance and State Control: The Total Information Awareness Project*, Basingstoke (UK), Palgrave Macmillan, 2010, 258 pp., Keith Laidler, *Surveillance Unlimited: How We've Become the Most Watched People on Earth*, Cambridge, Icon Books, 2008, 256 pp.

32. Joan Esteban, Laura Mayoral and Debraj Ray, "Ethnicity and Conflict: Theory and Facts," *Science*, New York, May 18, 2012, vol. 336, pp. 858–865.

33. Cf. http://www.arche-de-st-antoine.com/communaute/non violence/.

34. The Invisible Committee, *The Coming Insurrection*, Massachusetts, Semiotext(e)/MIT Press, 2009, 135 pp. The original 2007 edition was published in France by Éditions La Fabrique. There is a Spanish edition published by Melusina (2009).

35. Ivan Arreguín-Toft, "How the Weak Win Wars: A Theory of Asymmetric Conflict," New York, *International Security* 26:1, p. 100. The analysis cited is found in this work.

36. Jake Hartigan, *Why the Weak Win Wars: A Study of the Factors that Drive Strategy in Asymmetric Conflict*, dissertation, Monterrey (CA), Naval Postgraduate School, 79 pp.

37. In the words of Gandhi: "The British want us to put the struggle on the plane of machine-guns where they have the weapons and we do not. Our only assurance of beating them is putting the struggle on a plane where we have the weapons and they have not." Quoted in *Freedom at Midnight*, Dominique Lapierre and Larry Collins, 1997, Vikas, New Dehli, p. 61. This implies a clear conviction of the value of asymmetry. Cf. http://noviolencia-activa .blogspot.mx/2006/05/gandhi-y-king.html. Some theorists of nonviolence, such as Jean Goss and Jean Marie Müller, tend to reverse the strategy and tactics of war under a pacifist logic: http://noviolencia-activa.blogspot.mx/2006/05/metodologia-de-la -no-violencia-activa. html. The genealogy of the pacifist doctrine emanates from Jainism and the principle of "ahisma" (cause no injury), Evangelical Christianity, the civil disobedience of Henry David Thoreau, the austerity of John Ruskin and the Christian anarchism of Tolstoy, among other sources. Many of these pacifists seem to nevertheless accept the Latin rule *Arma in armatos sumere jura sinunt*, the laws permit the taking up of arms against the armed.

38. Leon E. Panetta, Remarks by Secretary Panetta at King's College London, January 18, 2013: http://archive.defense.gov /transcripts/transcript.aspx?transcriptid=5180. The military process aims to be irreversible.

ABOUT THE AUTHORS

Sergio González Rodríguez (1950–2017) was a writer, journalist, and critic for the Mexico City newspaper *Reforma*. His works include *The Iguala 43* and *The Femicide Machine* (both published by Semiotext(e)).

David Lida is the author, most recently, of the novel *One Life*.